AF560282

1. Cheese Factories
2. Angorat International Airport
3. Comic Book Store
4. Mouse General Hospital
5. WRAT Radio & Television Station
6. Snotnose Castle
7. Cheese Market
8. Grand Hotel
9. Botanical Gardens
10. Petunia Pretty Paws's House
11. *The Daily Rat*
12. *The Rodent's Gazette*
13. Thea's House
14. Cheap Junk for Less
15. Geronimo's House
16. Benjamin's House
17. Public Library
18. Mousidon Square Garden
19. Hercule Poirat's Office
20. New Mouse Harbor
21. Beach
22. Curlyfur Island Amousement Park
23. Shipyard
24. Luna Light House
25. The Statue of Liberty

Geronimo Stilton

THE GRAPHIC NOVEL

SLIME FOR DINNER

with
Tom Angleberger

story by
Elisabetta Dami

color by Corey Barba

graphix

An Imprint of

SCHOLASTIC

Published by Scholastic Inc., *Publishers since 1920*, 557 Broadway, New York, NY 10012. SCHOLASTIC and associated logos are trademarks and/or registered trademarks of Scholastic Inc.

Stilton is the name of a famous English cheese. It is a registered trademark of the Stilton Cheese Makers' Association. For more information, go to stiltoncheese.com.

"National Anthem of the Sewers" adapted and composed by Oscar Angleberger

ISBN 978-93-9059-013-1

Text by Geronimo Stilton
Story by Elisabetta Dami
Original title *Cena Con Mistero*
Cover and Illustrations by Tom Angleberger
Edited by Abigail McAden and Tiffany Colón
Translated by Emily Clement
Color by Corey Barba
Lettering by Kristin Kemper
Book design by Phil Falco and Shivana Sookdeo
Creative Director: Phil Falco
Publisher: David Saylor

First edition, February 2021

This reprint edition, August 2023

Printed in India at Polykam Offset, Naraina, New Delhi - 110028

TABLE OF

CONTENTS

Ah... What a beautiful day!

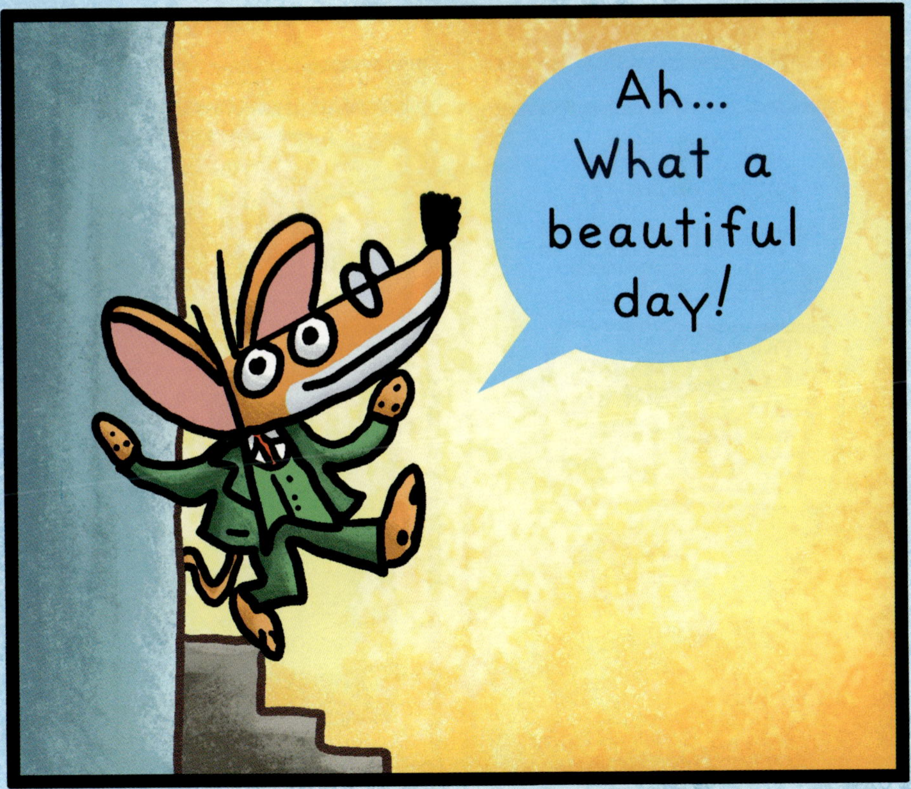

Oh, I forgot to introduce myself... My name is Stilton...

Geronimo Stilton!

I'm the publisher of THE RODENT'S GAZETTE.
THE RODENT'S GAZETTE
SAFE TO COME BACK
But, I'm also writing a novel. Its title will be...

OUTTA THE WAY, BUB!

No, that's not the name of my novel! That's what a truck driver was yelling!

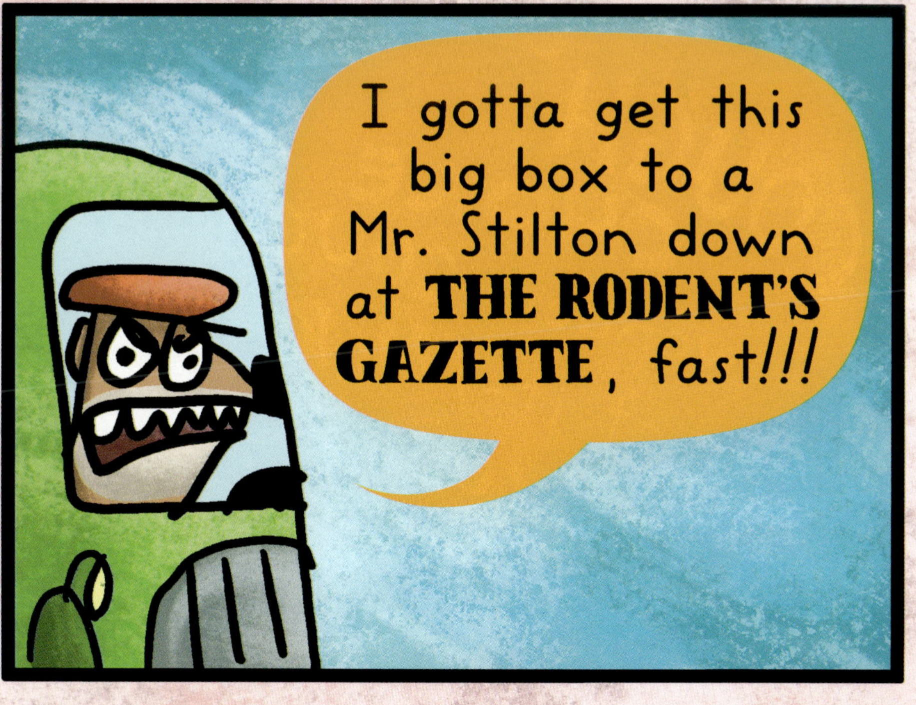

I gotta get this big box to a Mr. Stilton down at **THE RODENT'S GAZETTE**, fast!!!

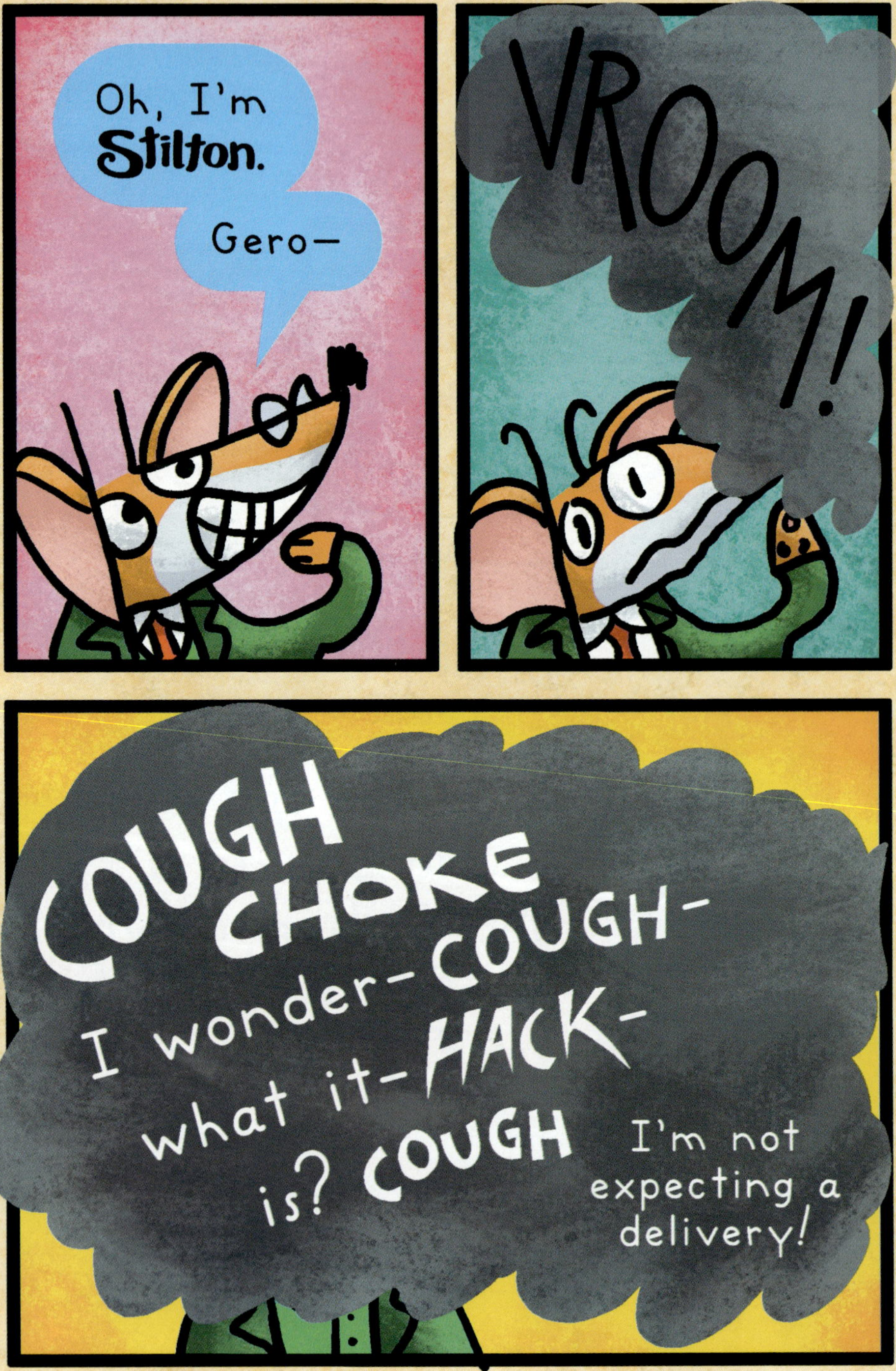

COUGH
CHOKE
I wonder-COUGH-what it-HACK-is? COUGH
I'm not expecting a delivery!

By the time I got to my office, the box had been delivered.

And my secretary, Mousella MacMouser, was FRANTIC!

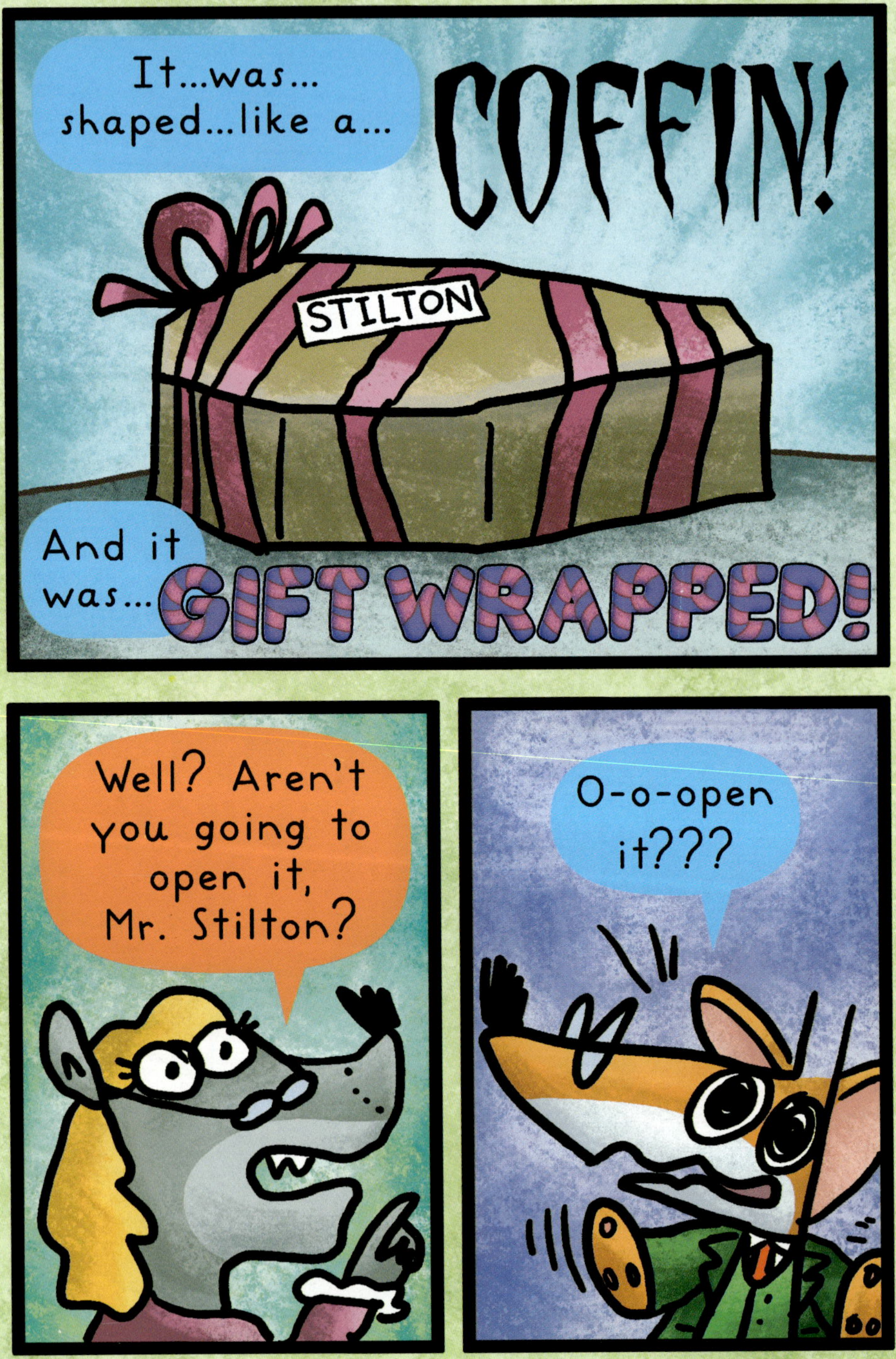

It...was... shaped...like a...

COFFIN!

STILTON

And it was... GIFT WRAPPED!

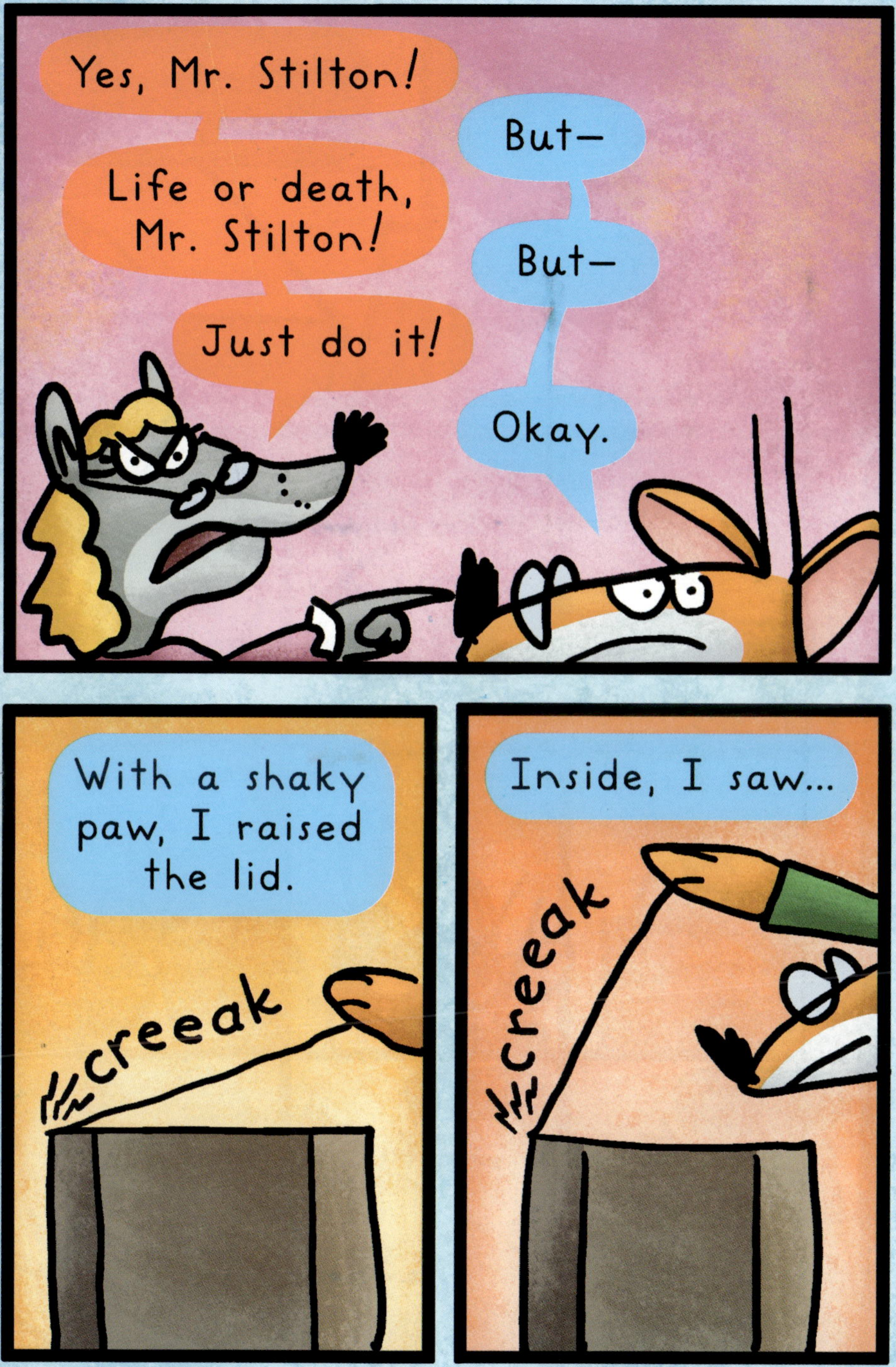

Yes, Mr. Stilton!

But—

Life or death, Mr. Stilton!

But—

Just do it!

Okay.

Another box!

And inside that was...

And inside that was...
And inside that was...
I don't have time for this!
And inside that was...
I'm a busy mouse!
And inside that was...
And inside that was...
And inside that was...
Why me?

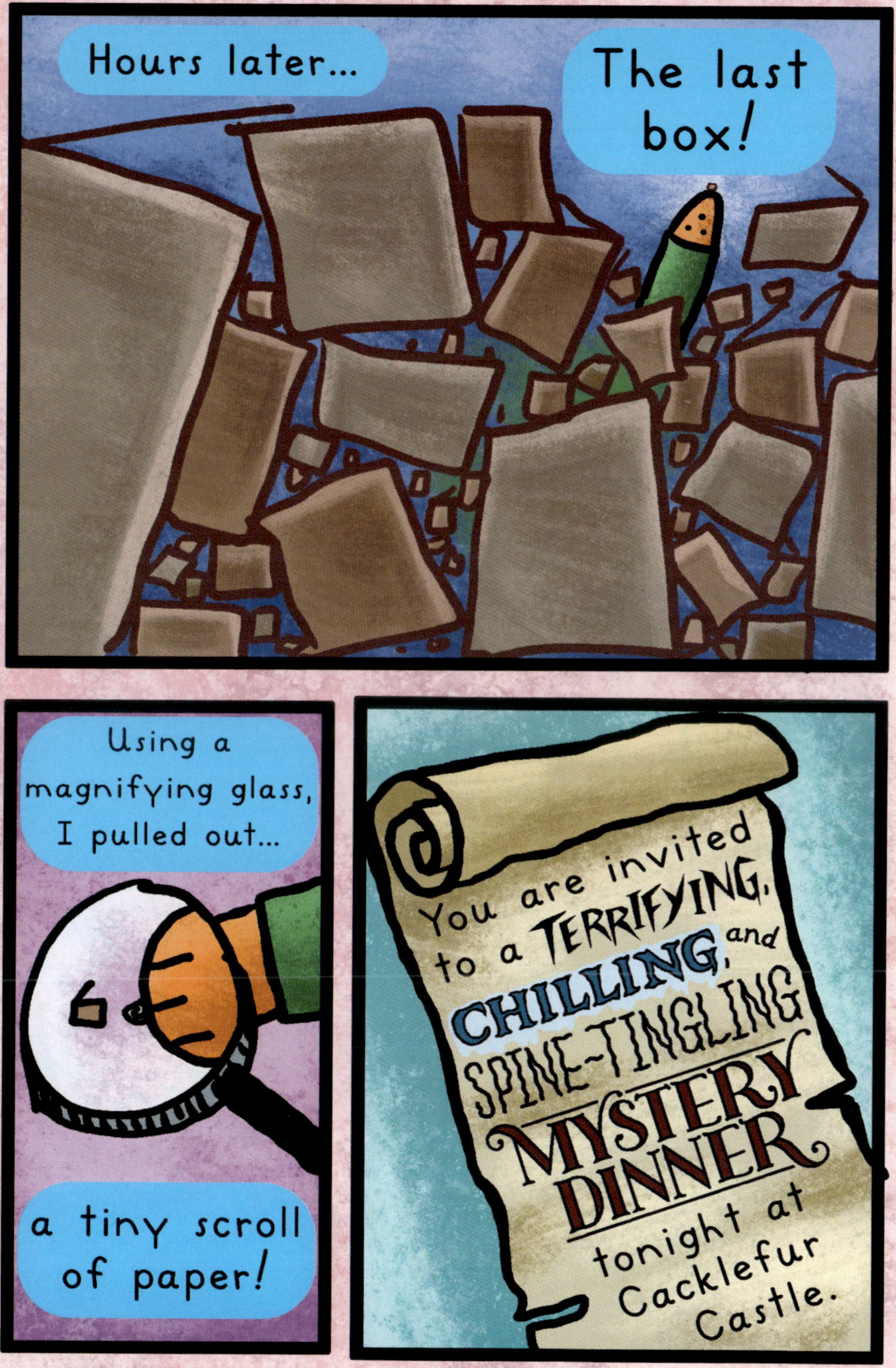

Hours later...

The last box!

CHAPTER TWO
READY, GERRY?

A mystery dinner?! Sounds fabumouse, Mr. Stilton!

I think it sounds terrible, and I don't even know what it is!

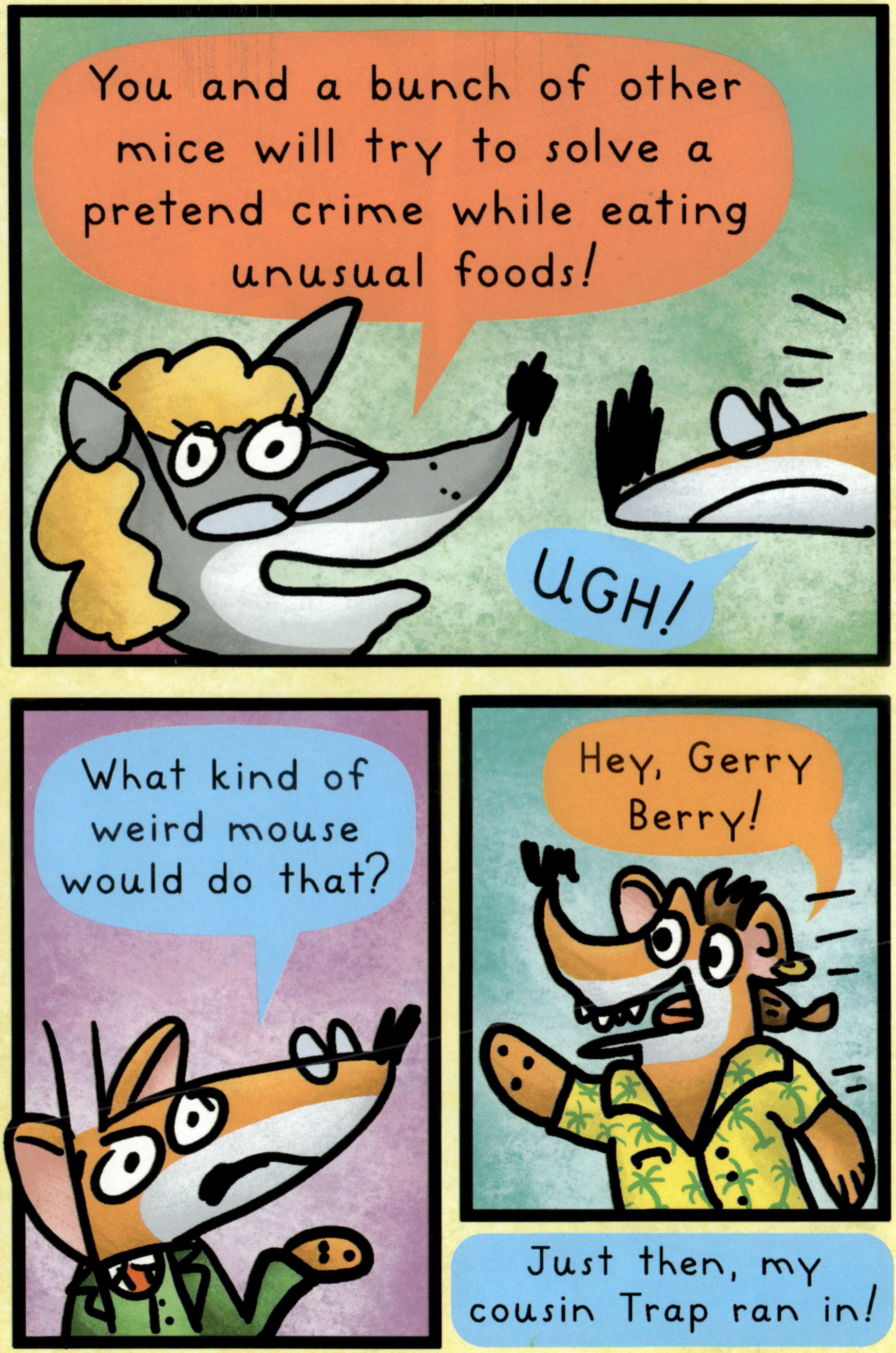

You and a bunch of other mice will try to solve a pretend crime while eating unusual foods!

UGH!

Just then, my cousin Trap ran in!

Please don't call me that. My name is Stilton, Ger—

No time, Cuz! We gotta go! You're late!

Late for what?

For the mystery dinner!

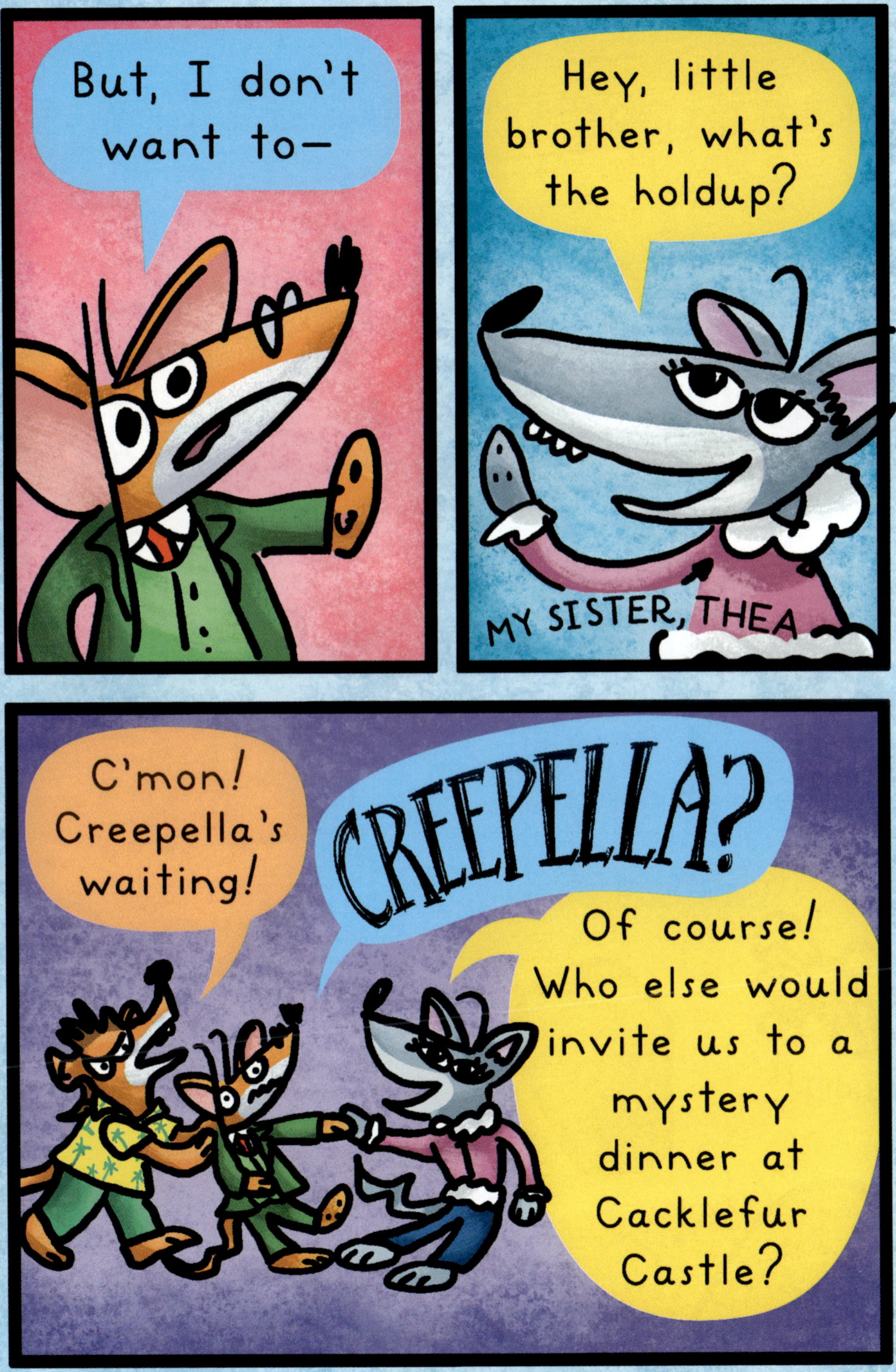

C'mon! Creepella's waiting!

CREEPELLA?

Of course! Who else would invite us to a mystery dinner at Cacklefur Castle?

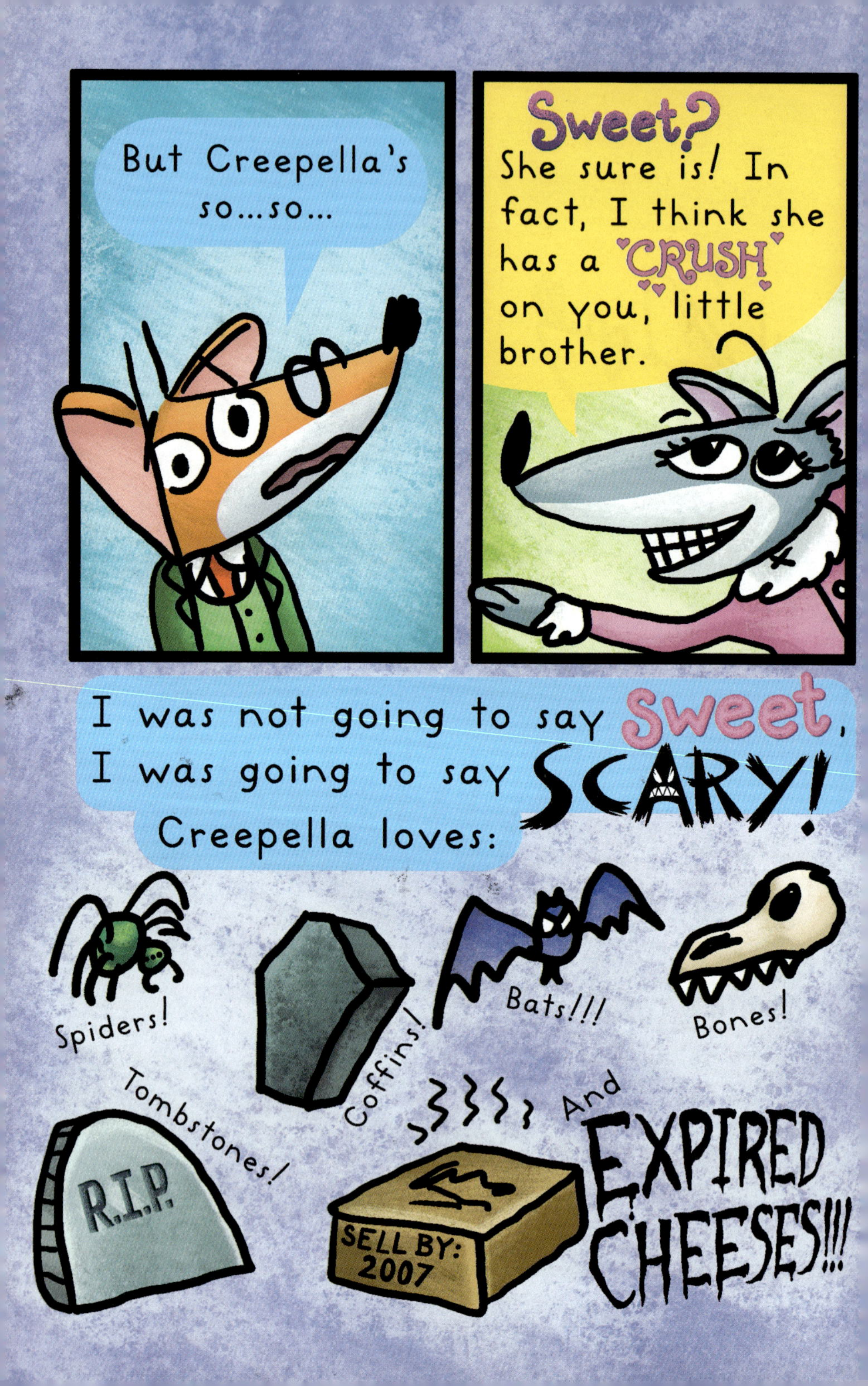

I was not going to say Sweet, I was going to say SCARY!

Creepella loves:

Spiders!

Coffins!

Bats!!!

Bones!

Tombstones!

R.I.P.

SELL BY: 2007

And EXPIRED CHEESES!!!

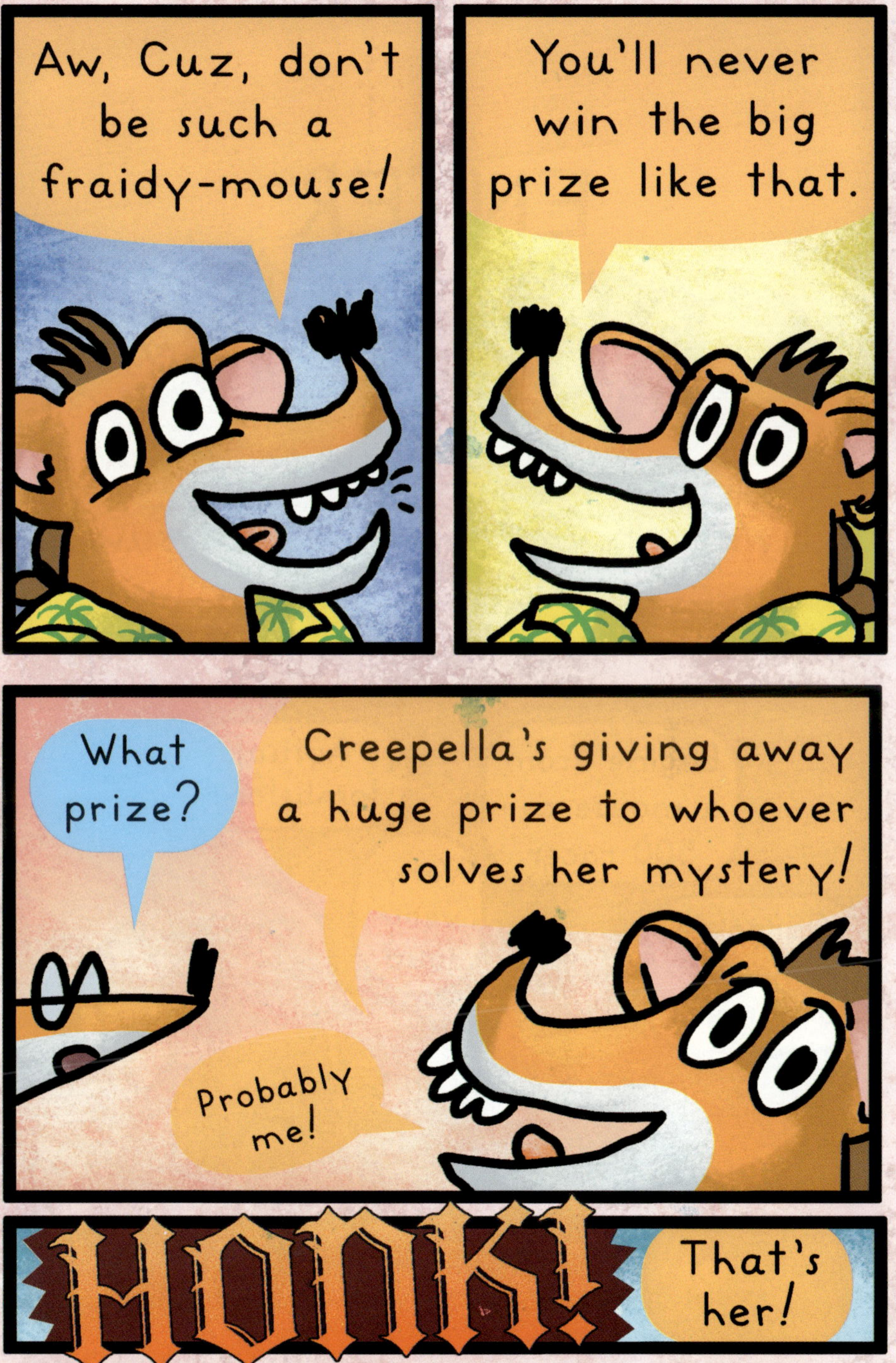

What prize?

Creepella's giving away a huge prize to whoever solves her mystery!

Probably me!

HONK!

That's her!

CHAPTER THREE

ENTER CREEPELLA

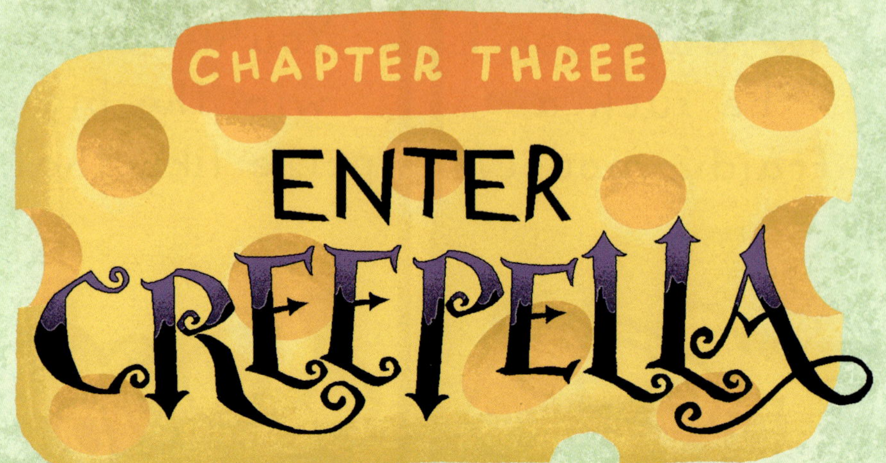

We ran downstairs and saw Creepella waiting for us in her car, the TURBO-TOMBSTONE!

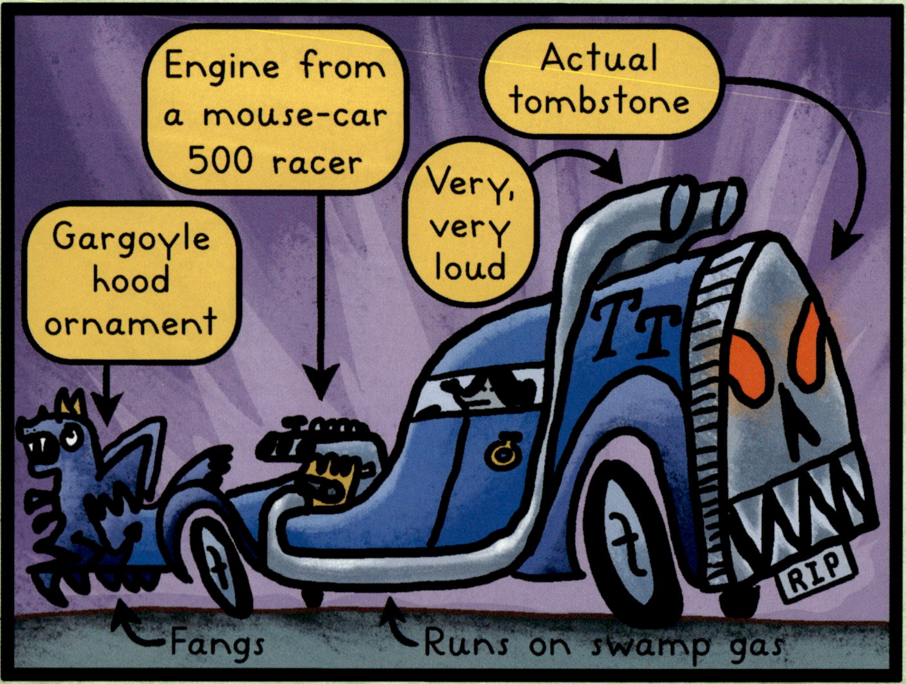
Engine from a mouse-car 500 racer
Actual tombstone
Very, very loud
Gargoyle hood ornament
TT
RIP
Fangs
Runs on swamp gas

YOOHOO, GERRYKINS!
Thea! Trap!
Hop in! Cacklefur Castle awaits!

Trap and I tried to squeeze into the back seat while Thea and Creepella chatted up front...

VROOM!
TT

Creepella drove like a bat out of Havarti* up the CURVY roads!
SCREECH
NEW MOUSE CITY
CACKLEFUR CASTLE
MYSTERIOUS VALLEY
*Havarti is a kind of cheese.

Creepella drove way too fast up the curvy mountain road!

Creepella... please...for cheddar's sake...just SLOW DOWN!

Sorry, Gerrykins! I want to get there before moonrise! It'll be a FULL MOON! So pretty!

Somehow, we arrived alive. Creepella screeched to a halt, and I stumbled out of the car.

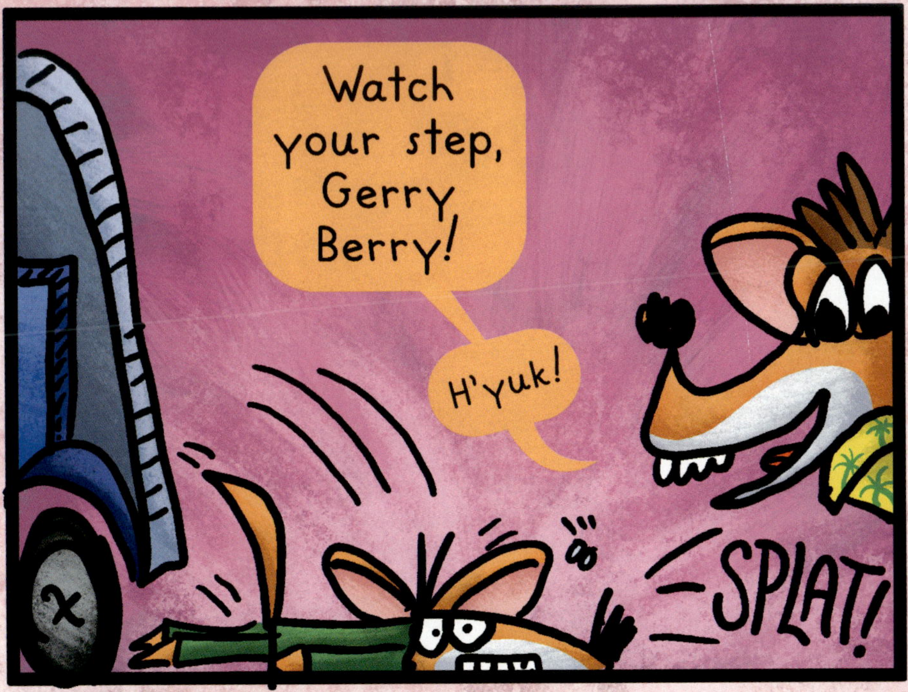

Watch your step, Gerry Berry!
H'yuk!
SPLAT!

I thought Creepella's driving was scary... But her home was even worse. Much worse!

Oh, Gerrykins... Isn't it a lovely night?
Lovely?! More like TERRIFYING!

You're so silly! The scares are all for fun! A mystery dinner is just a game!
Nothing's going to hurt you! 
GRRRRR...

CHAPTER FIVE

OH, WHAT A TANGLED WEB

When we got inside, it was even scarier than it had been outside!

Like it?
I hated it!!
It was SO CREEPY!
There were scary swords...
razor-sharp axes...
a golden coffin...
drippy candles...
...and spiderwebs everywhere!

I tried to offer some helpful advice...

Maybe we should clean up some of these webs before the dinner...

YOW!

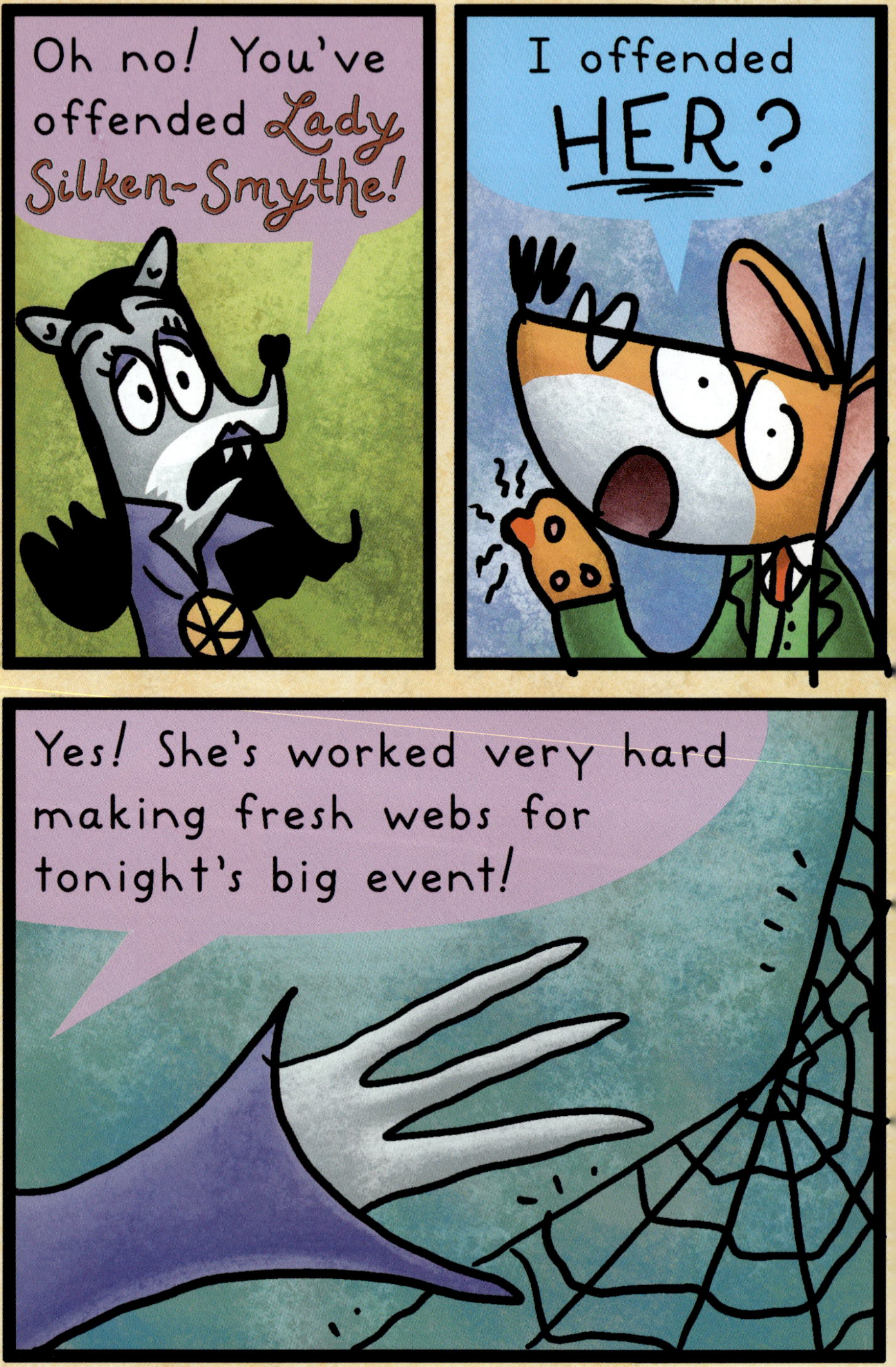

Yes! She's worked very hard making fresh webs for tonight's big event!

Oh dear! She's scuttling off to her little closet!

scuttle scuttle

You'll have to send her a letter of apology!

SLAM

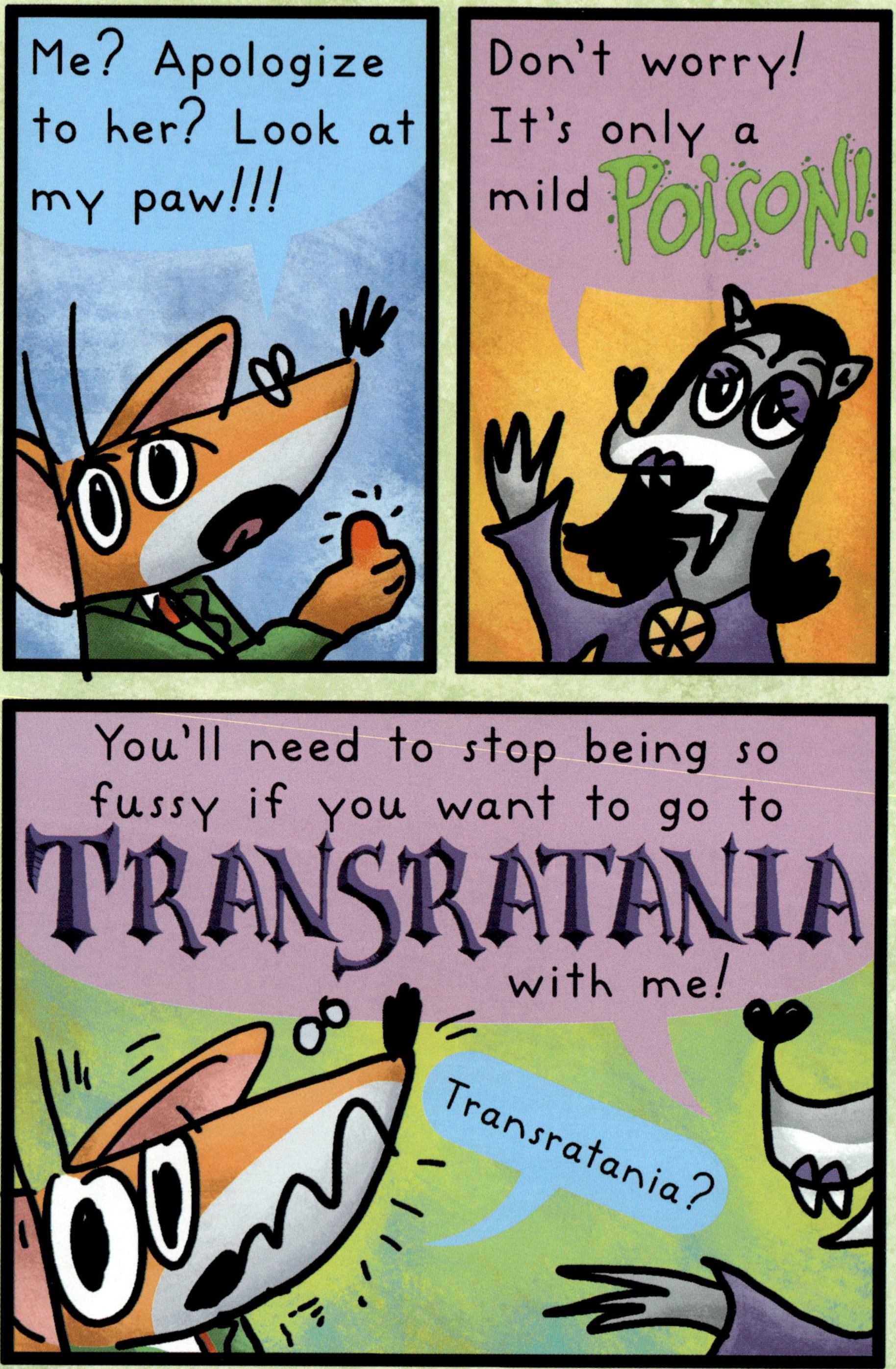

You'll need to stop being so fussy if you want to go to TRANSRATANIA with me!

Transratania?

Yes! That's the prize tonight! Whoever is **BRAVE**, ***DARING***, and **CLEVER** enough to solve the mystery will go with me to explore **TRANSRATANIA!**

I hope it's you, Gerry, because—

Just then, a huge **BAT** swooped in! It was Creepella's pet, Bitewing. And for once, I was happy to see him!

CHAPTER SIX

WHISKER-LICKIN' GOOOOOD!

Bitewing had brought Creepella a note...

I was glad! Giuseppe's food is always so GROSS!

Example: fungus and dumplings in mold sauce.

But it didn't look so good when we got to the kitchen! In fact, it looked like

SLIME!

Tonight's menu is all TRANSRATANIAN food!!

I want to prove I am the best one to go on the trip with you, CREEPELLA!

Here, taste some!

It was FOUL!
It was DISGUSTING!
It tasted like TOAD SLIME!

That made Boffo very happy and Trap mad...

GRRRRR-
RRRRRR-
RRRRRR!

GRRRRRRRR-
WHOOPS!

CRUSTY* MUENSTER CLUMPS!
WHY ME?
*Muenster is a kind of cheese.

I was mad! I was angry!
I was covered in
SLIME
from head to tail!

Then it got worse!!!

CHOMP

Sorry, Gerrykins!

I guess my pet flytrap, Chompers, couldn't resist.

I'm going home to take a shower!

Oh no! Don't do that, Gerrykins! It'll ruin my mystery dinner!

I CAN'T GO ON LIKE THIS!
Who?

I know! You can shower here! I'll have Snip + Snap show you the way!

CHAPTER SEVEN

NOT AS SWEET AS THEY LOOK!

Creepella called her nephews Snip + Snap to show me the way to the shower.

Creepella's adorable nephews led me through a door into a garden...

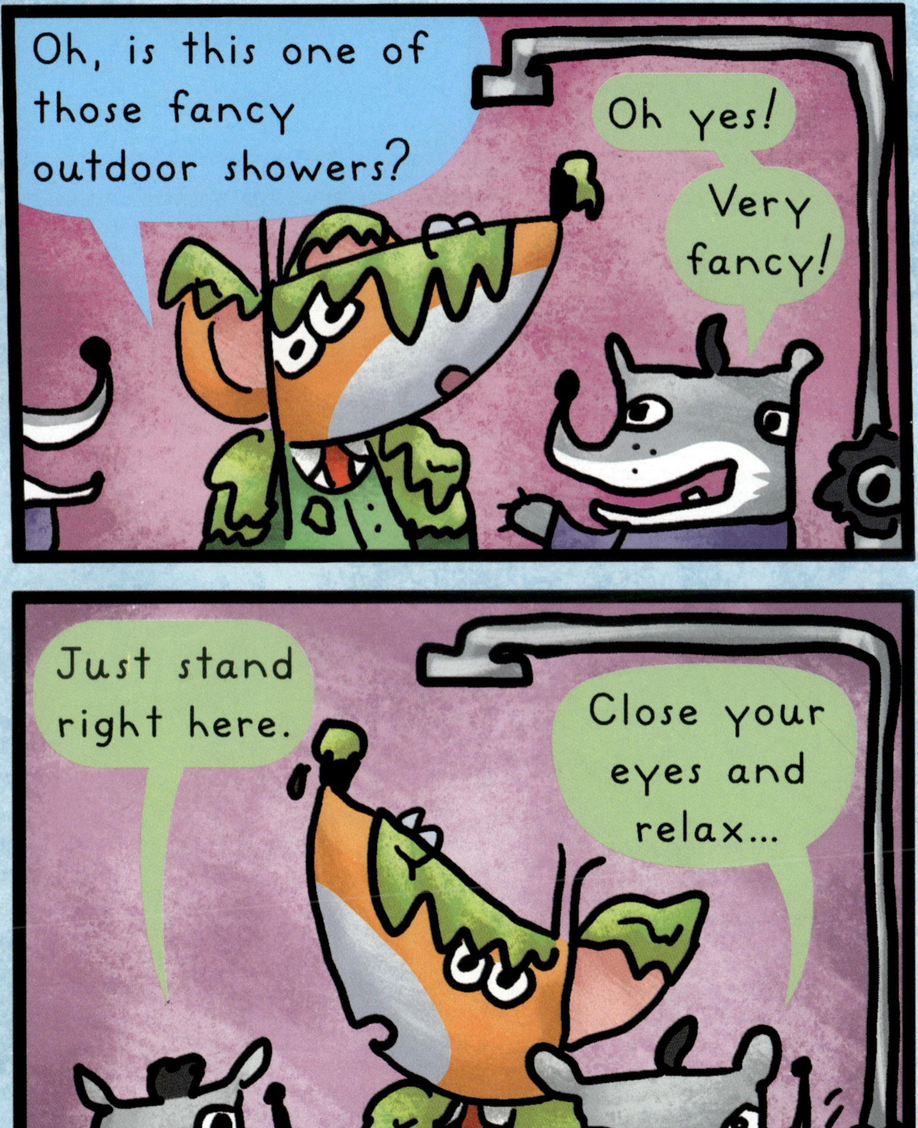

Just stand right here.

Close your eyes and relax...

SPLA-WOOSH!

HELP! SLUGS! NO!
SLUGS!
HELP!
WHY ME?
OH NOOOOO!
NO!
SLUGS!!!!
ACK!
CREEPELLA!!!
SOMEBODY GET THESE CREEPY SLUGS OFF ME!
HELP!
HA! HA! HA! HA!
HA! HA! HA! HA!

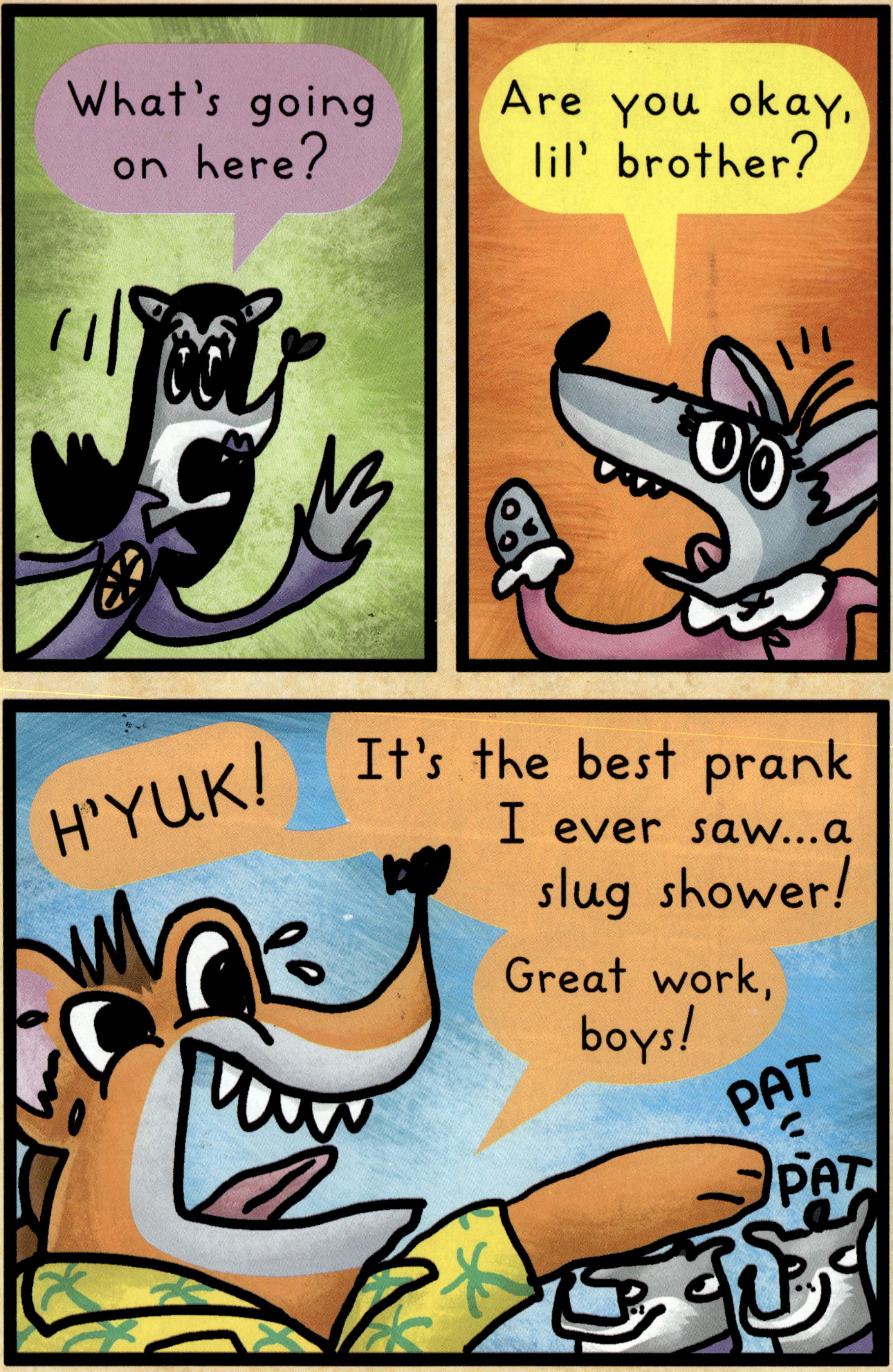

H'YUK!

It's the best prank I ever saw...a slug shower!

Great work, boys!

PAT

PAT

Tut, tut... How can a grown mouse be so worked up about a few werewolf slugs?

WERE WOLF SLUGS?!?!

Everyone knows they're harmless unless it's MIDNIGHT during a FULL MOON!

But... but...

TONIGHT IS A FULL MOON!

AWOOOOOO

Don't worry, I'm sure the boys will have all the slugs back in their cages by midnight...

Right, boys?

Oh, of course, Auntie dear!

Now, Gerry, you really must get cleaned up! The mystery dinner starts soon!

You look AWFUL, and not in a good way.

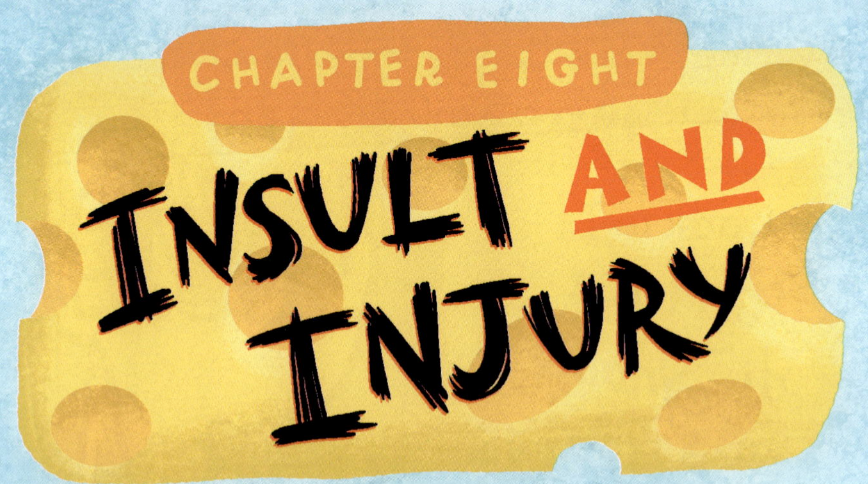

CHAPTER EIGHT
INSULT AND INJURY

Creepella said that since her grandfather had already gone to bed, I could use his bathtub...

It was CREEPY, but at least I could get CLEAN.

By the time I got dressed, another guest had arrived...

Look! It's Rattata di Snobizzi, the famouse **MYSTERY NOVELIST!**

Yoo-hoo, Creepella!

I've come to solve your mystery game with my amazing cleverness!

Are these the other guests?

:SNIFF:

They won't be much competition. We may as well leave on our trip now, Creepella.

HEY!

Are you callin' us dumb?

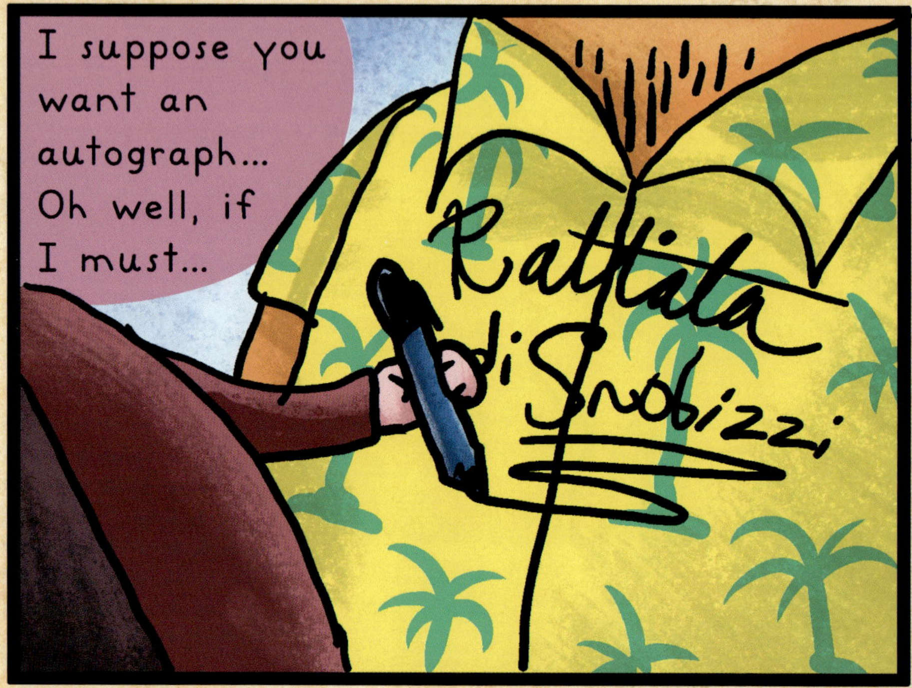

I suppose you want an autograph... Oh well, if I must...

Rattata diSnobizzi

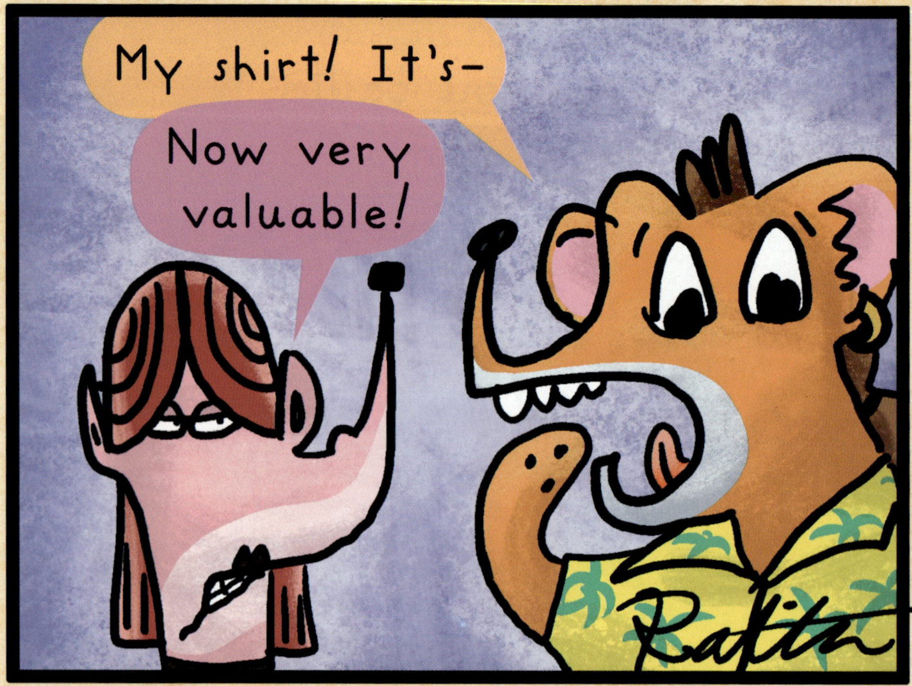

My shirt! It's-

Now very valuable!

I suppose the rest of you all want my autograph, too?
SIGH

If I must...

Hold still!

Rattata
di

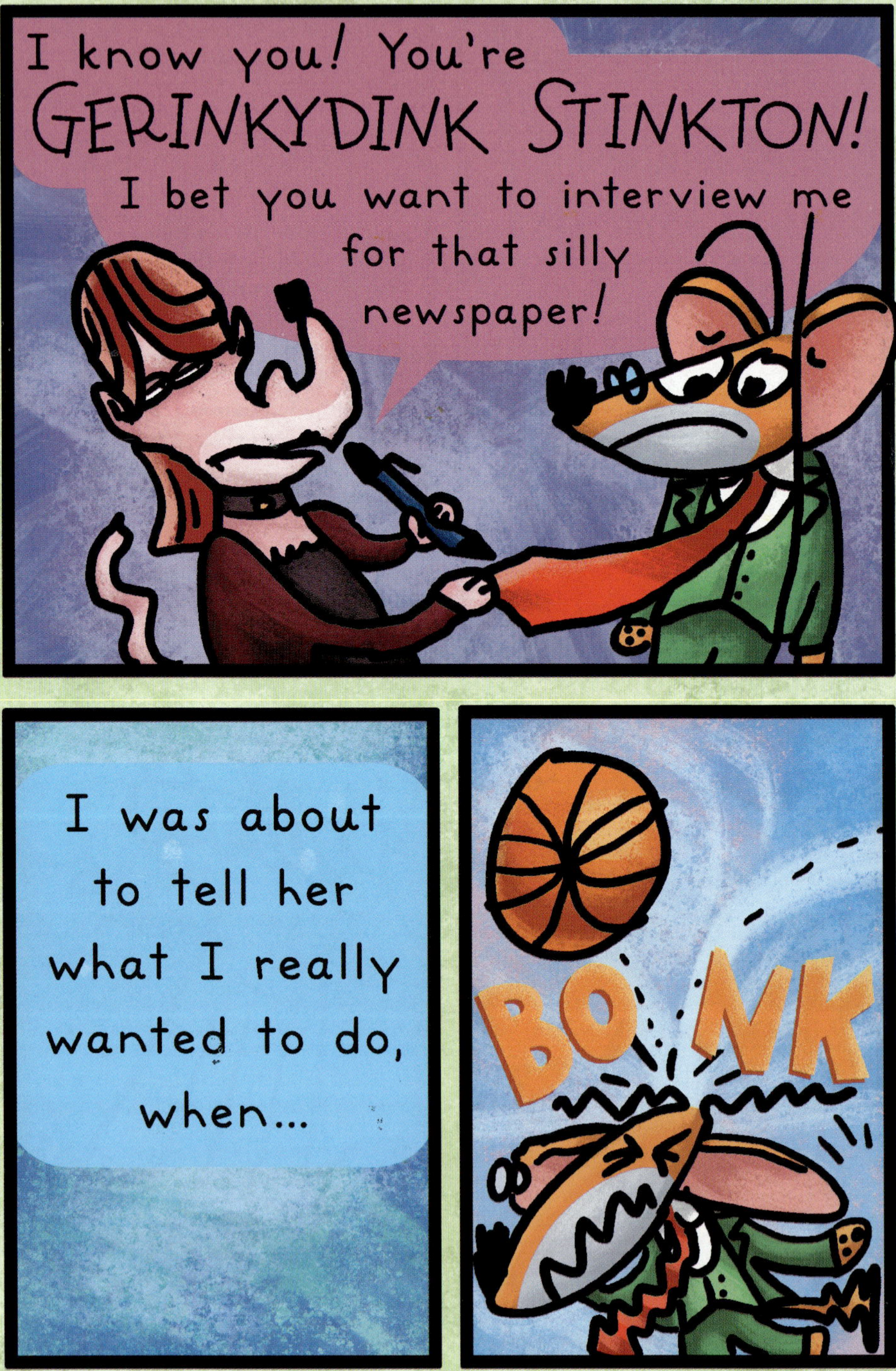

I know you! You're GERINKYDINK STINKTON! I bet you want to interview me for that silly newspaper!

I was about to tell her what I really wanted to do, when...

Everyone, meet our final guest, star of the Gloomies basketball team...

PERRY MISCUS!

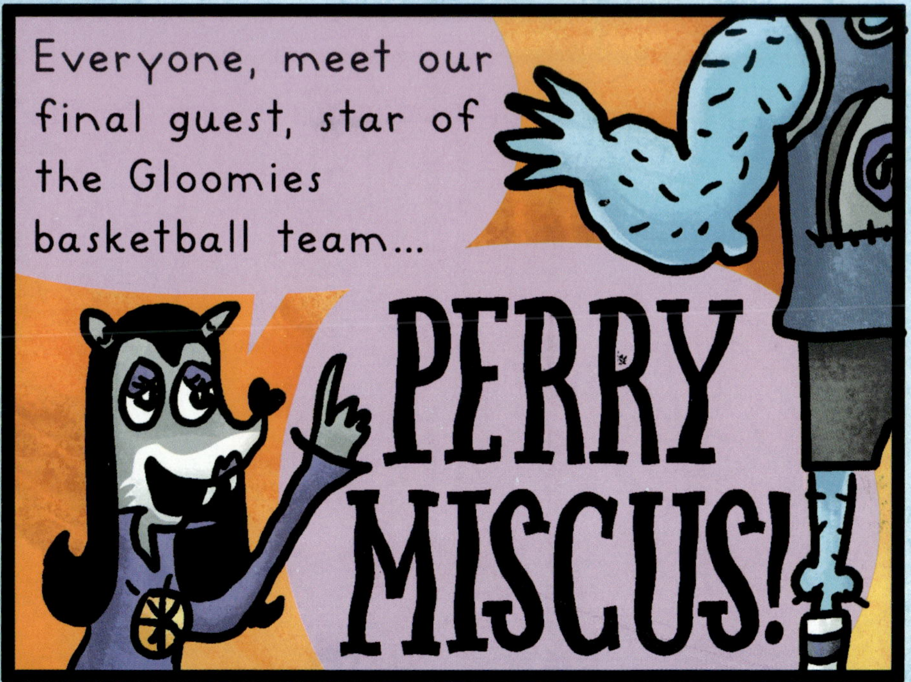

Creepella...
I made that perfect shot to prove I'll be the perfect teammate on our trip!

That "perfect" shot hit me on the head!

Yeah, like I said:

It was PERFECT!

Sorry, Cuz, that was my bad. H'yuk!

Say, that Perry is pretty cool, huh?

I'm really going to have to work hard to stay ahead!

CHAPTER TEN

THE OFFICIAL RULES

Just then, a coffin clock opened up, and a *SLUG* came out!

Eight o'clock!
Time for dinner!

Let the MYSTERY begin!

Uh... It will be over by midnight, right?

You just can't wait to win the prize, can you?

Well, I have it right here!

Two tickets to TRANSRATANIA!

One for me and one for... who?

ME!

ME!

ME!

ME!

me.

Psst! Gerry Berry! If I win, I'll give you the prize!

That's not necessary!

Anything for you, little brother!

Everyone, take your seats, and I'll go over the rules!

TRAP

BOB

CREEPELLA'S FIRST-EVER
MYSTERY DINNER
Official Rules and Guidelines

A puzzling crime has been made up for you to have FUN solving while eating fine foods!

1. Something has been "STOLEN." (Remem[...]r, it's not really stolen, but [...] all be pretending it was stolen.)

2. A chain of CLUES will help you find out what was stolen and where it has been hidden!

3. The rodent who recovers the "stolen" object WINS!

4. You're NOT allowed to ask ANY of the CACKLEFUR CASTLE ghosts for help!

The first clue is... written at the bottom of your soup bowl!
Eat fast to be the first to read it!

Enjoy, everyone! I made it from the freshest salamanders I could get!

It smells like SKUNK SQUIRTS! Who could possibly eat this!?!

I had thought the soup was the grossest thing ever... NO. Trap's soupy belch was! So let's move on to the next chapter!!!

CHAPTER ELEVEN

THE FIRST CLUE!

After his **REVOLTING** belch, Trap actually asked for more!

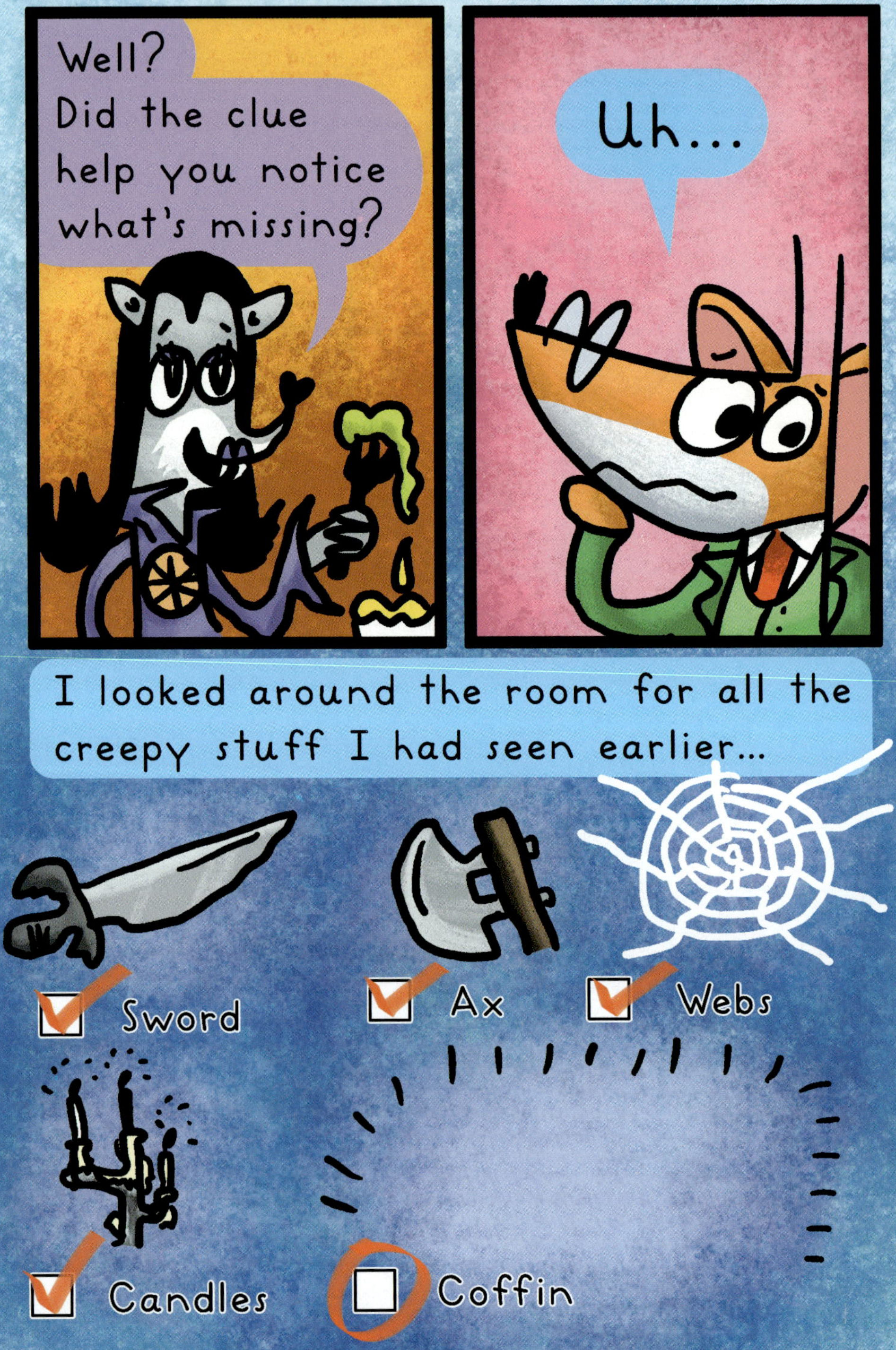

I looked around the room for all the creepy stuff I had seen earlier...

- [x] Sword
- [x] Ax
- [x] Webs
- [x] Candles
- [ ] Coffin

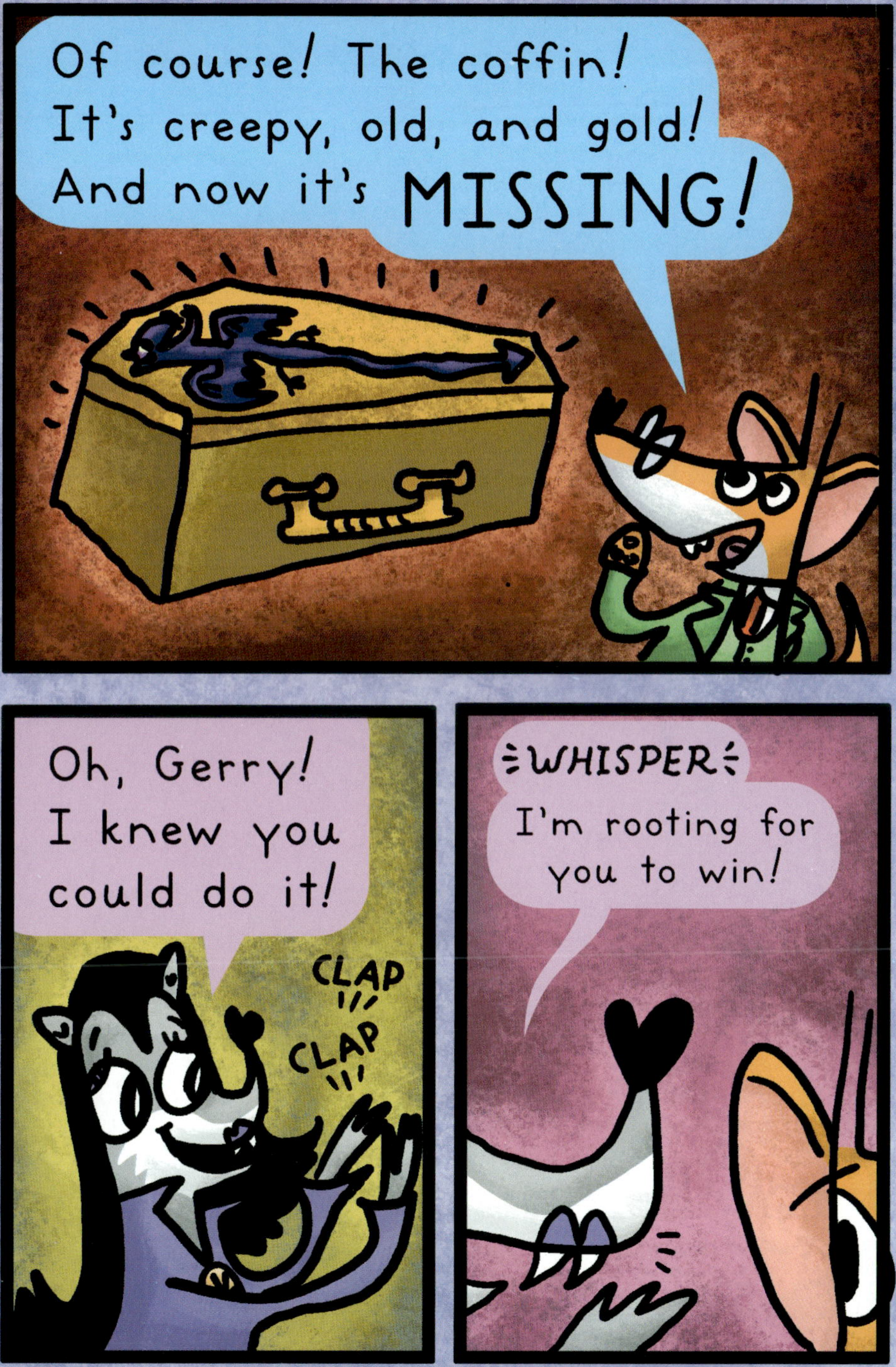

Of course! The coffin!
It's creepy, old, and gold!
And now it's MISSING!

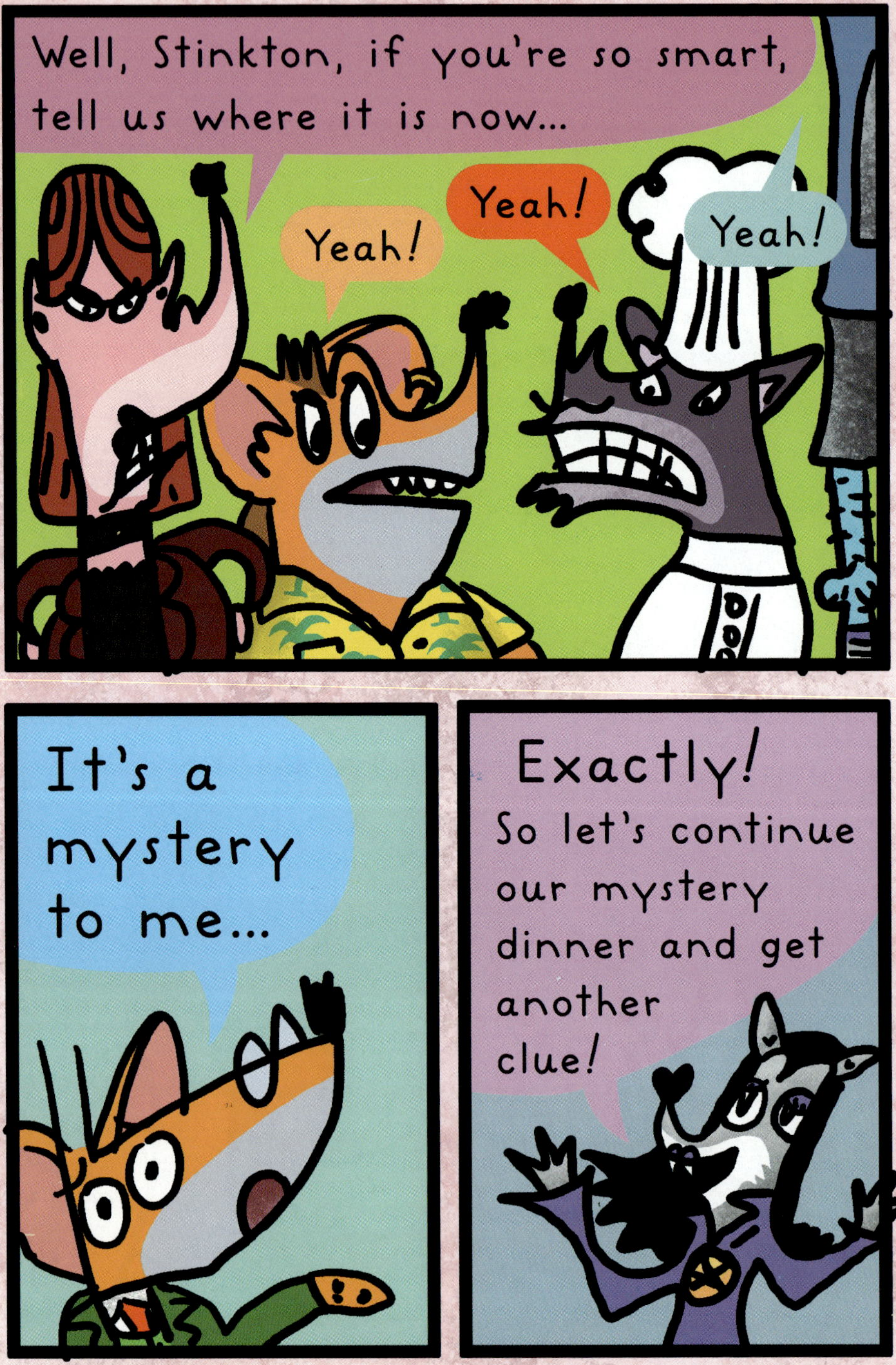

Well, Stinkton, if you're so smart, tell us where it is now...

Yeah!

Yeah!

Yeah!

CHAPTER TWELVE

THE SECOND CLUE!

We all sat down again, and Boffo served his next course...

RUNNY ROQUEFORT!*

It's REVOLTIN'!

*Roquefort is a kind of cheese.

Yummy yum

It's so moist!

Seconds, please!

Pssst, Gerry...
Notice anything weird about the food?

Uh...
Yes?

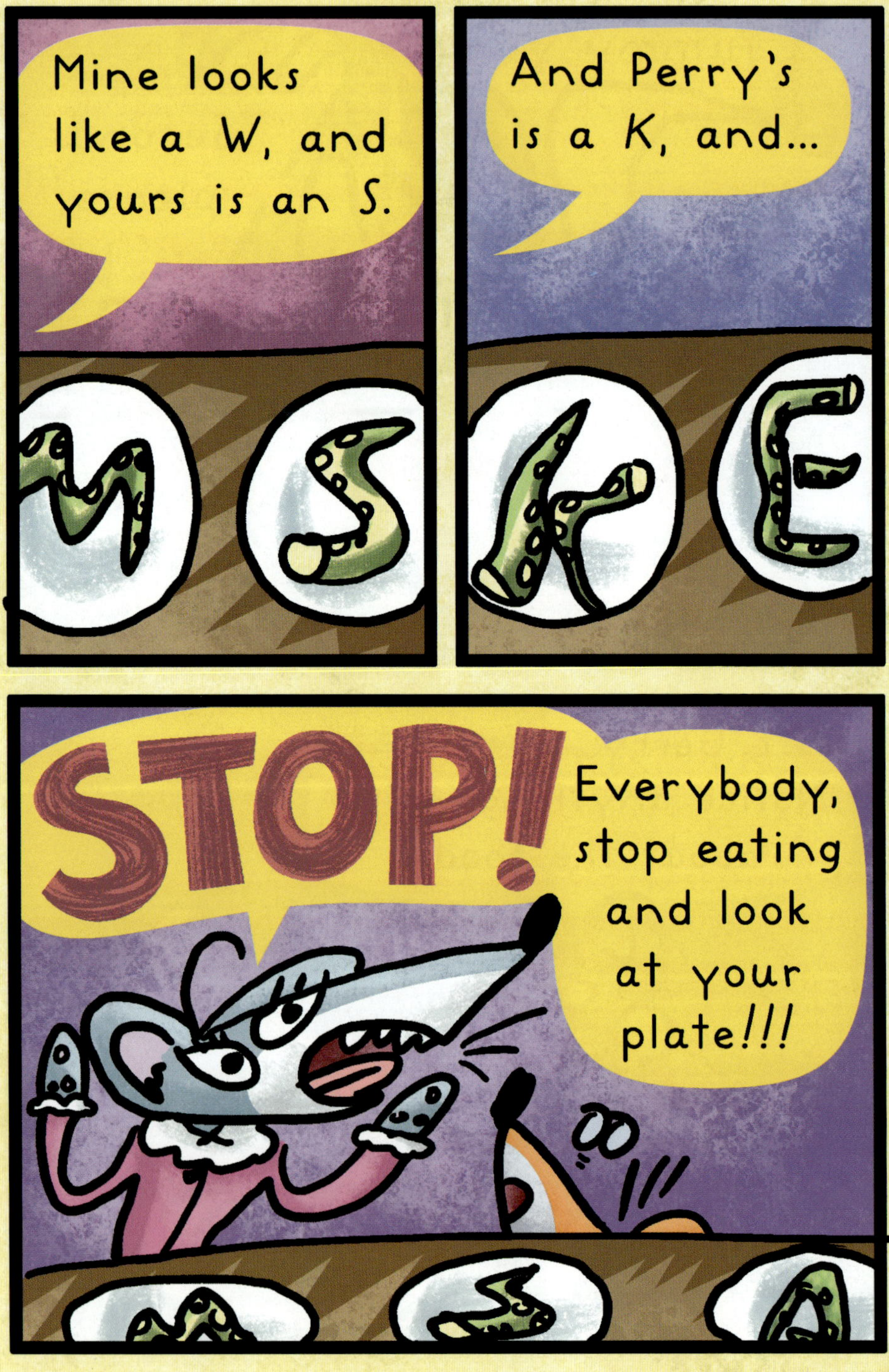

STOP!

Everybody, stop eating and look at your plate!!!

BAT'S-EYE VIEW
Each plate has a letter!
The food is the clue!

What about our plates?

Ours are a *P* and an *E*!

KIDS' TABLE →

Bring them over!

Let's clear away the silverware so we can arrange the letters into words!

"EW, PEE LEAKS?"
What kind of clue is that?

That is not the clue!

Thank goodness! I had enough of that in my last book!

But the letters don't really spell anything else!

We must be missing something!
But what?

H'yuk, h'yuk! You're missing the one I ate!

Of course! What shape was it?

Uh...
Kraken-shaped?

No, it was an *R*, as in *Rattata*!

Pssst... See if you can figure it out before the next page!

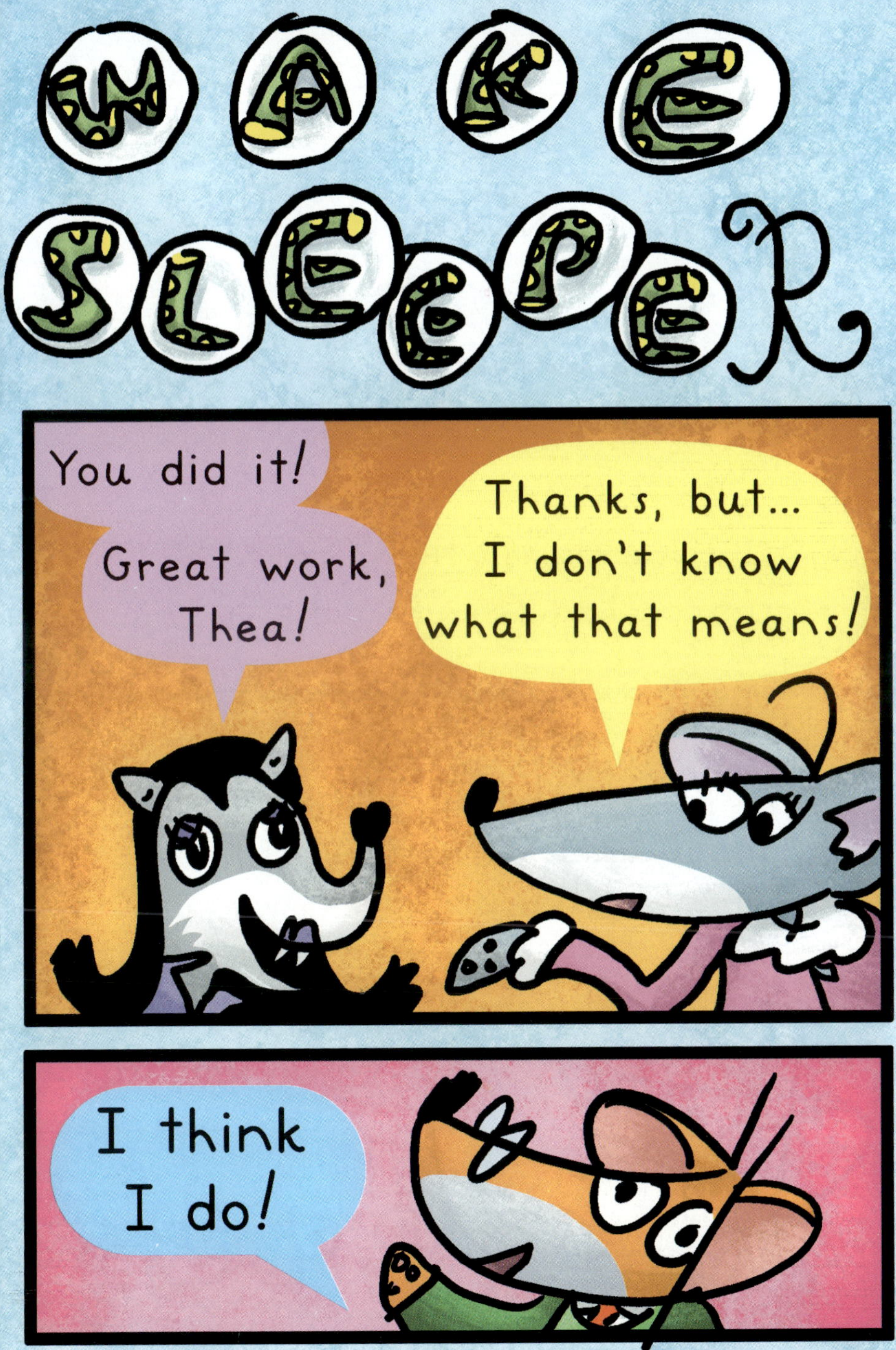

You did it!

Great work, Thea!

Thanks, but... I don't know what that means!

CHAPTER THIRTEEN

WAKING UP THE Sleeper

I remembered that Creepella's grandpa had already gone to bed.

When we got to his room, I could hear him snoring, but I couldn't see a thing!
GENTLE SNORE

Maybe you should flip on the light switch!

Oh... Thank you, Snip.
I'm Snap!
Oh... Sorry.
DANGER!!!
HIGH VOLTAGE

FLIP
DANGER
HIGH VOLTAGE

BZZT

RAWR!

I was TERRIFIED!

I was PETRIFIED!

EEK!

I was... wondering why Snip and Snap were laughing!

HA HA!

Ha ha ha!

Hee hee!

Did you see his face?

Hee hee!

What a scaredy-mouse!

Yuk yuk!

#wimp!

We got him good!

Let's tell Trap!

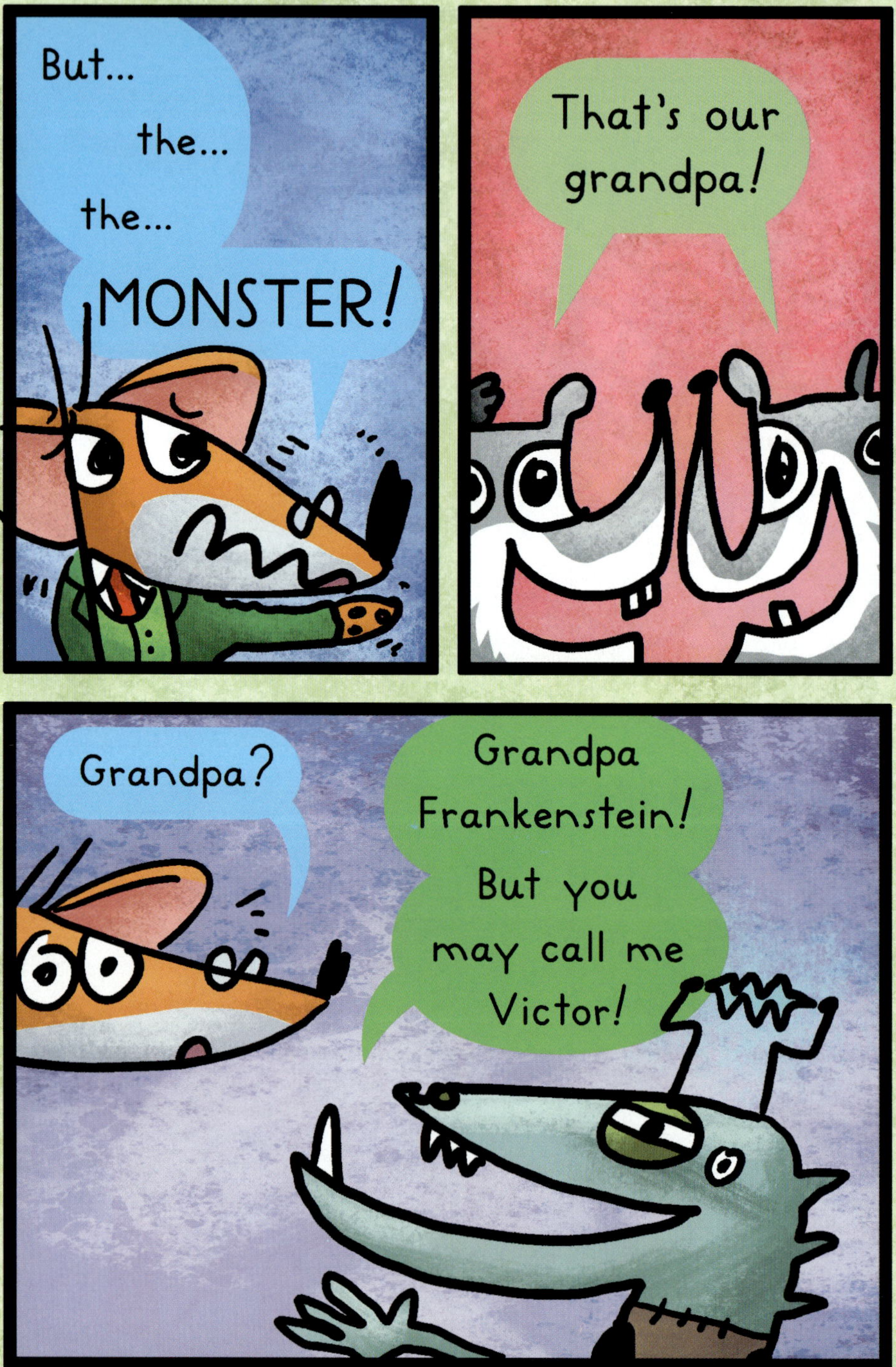

Grandpa?

Grandpa Frankenstein!

But you may call me Victor!

Victor Von Cacklefur stomped to the dining room and, I am happy to say, ate my leftovers...

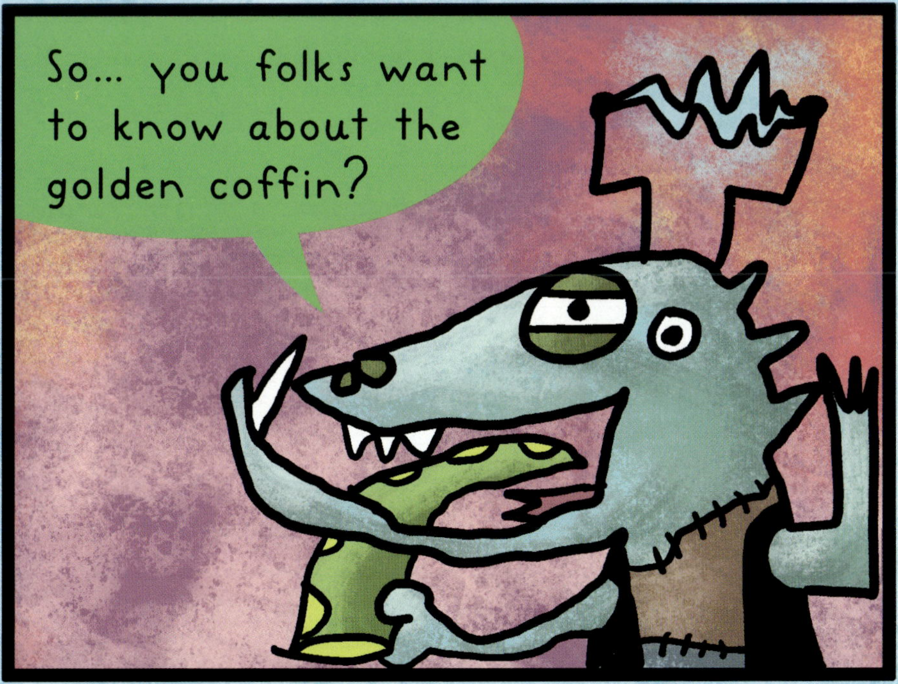

So... you folks want to know about the golden coffin?

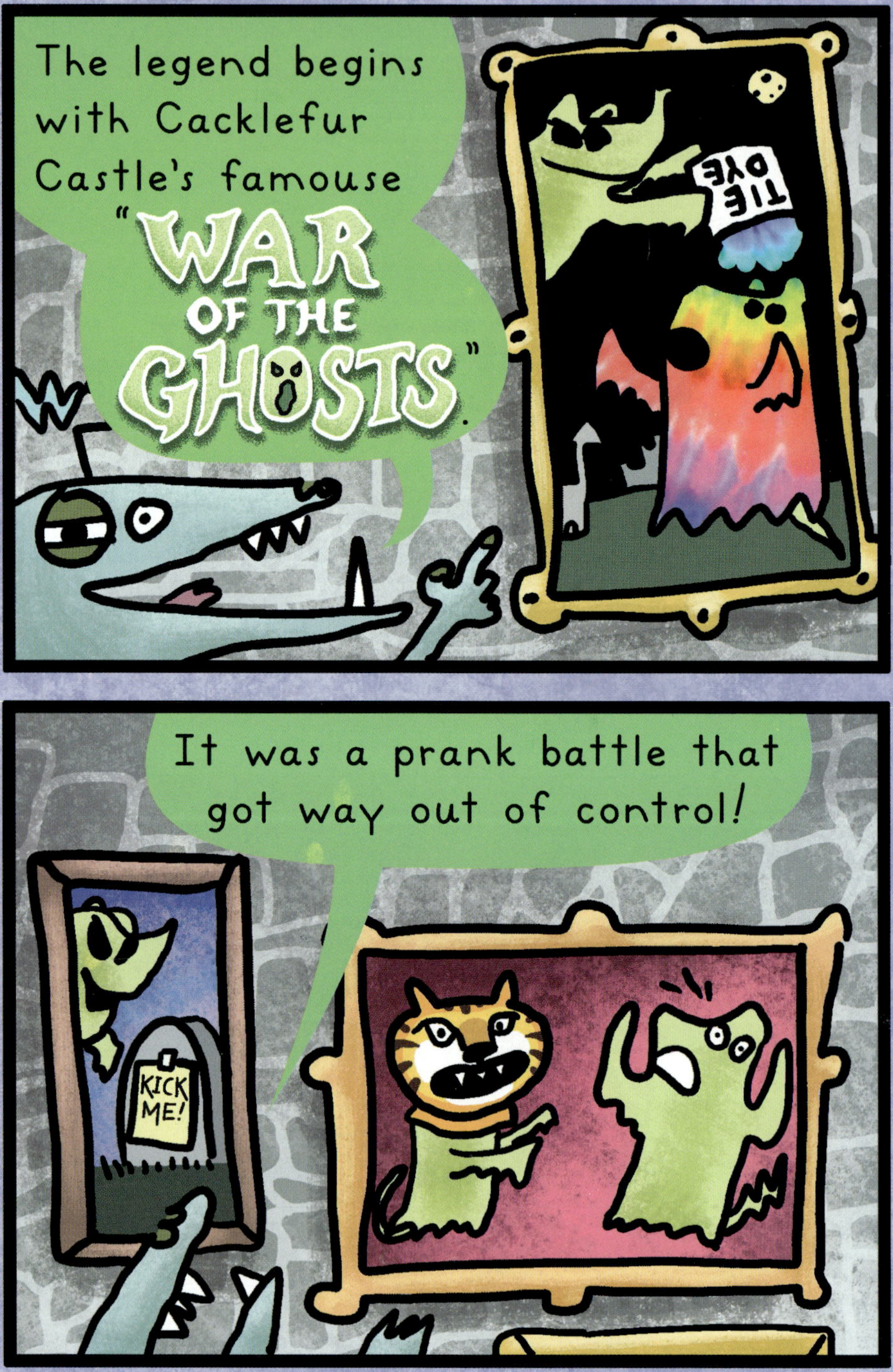

The legend begins with Cacklefur Castle's famouse "WAR OF THE GHOSTS".

It was a prank battle that got way out of control!

It did not sound awesome! Ghosts and pranks are two of my top five least favorite things!

My least favorite things:

1. Pranks
2. Ghosts
3. Folk music
4. Bad smells
5. Lima beans

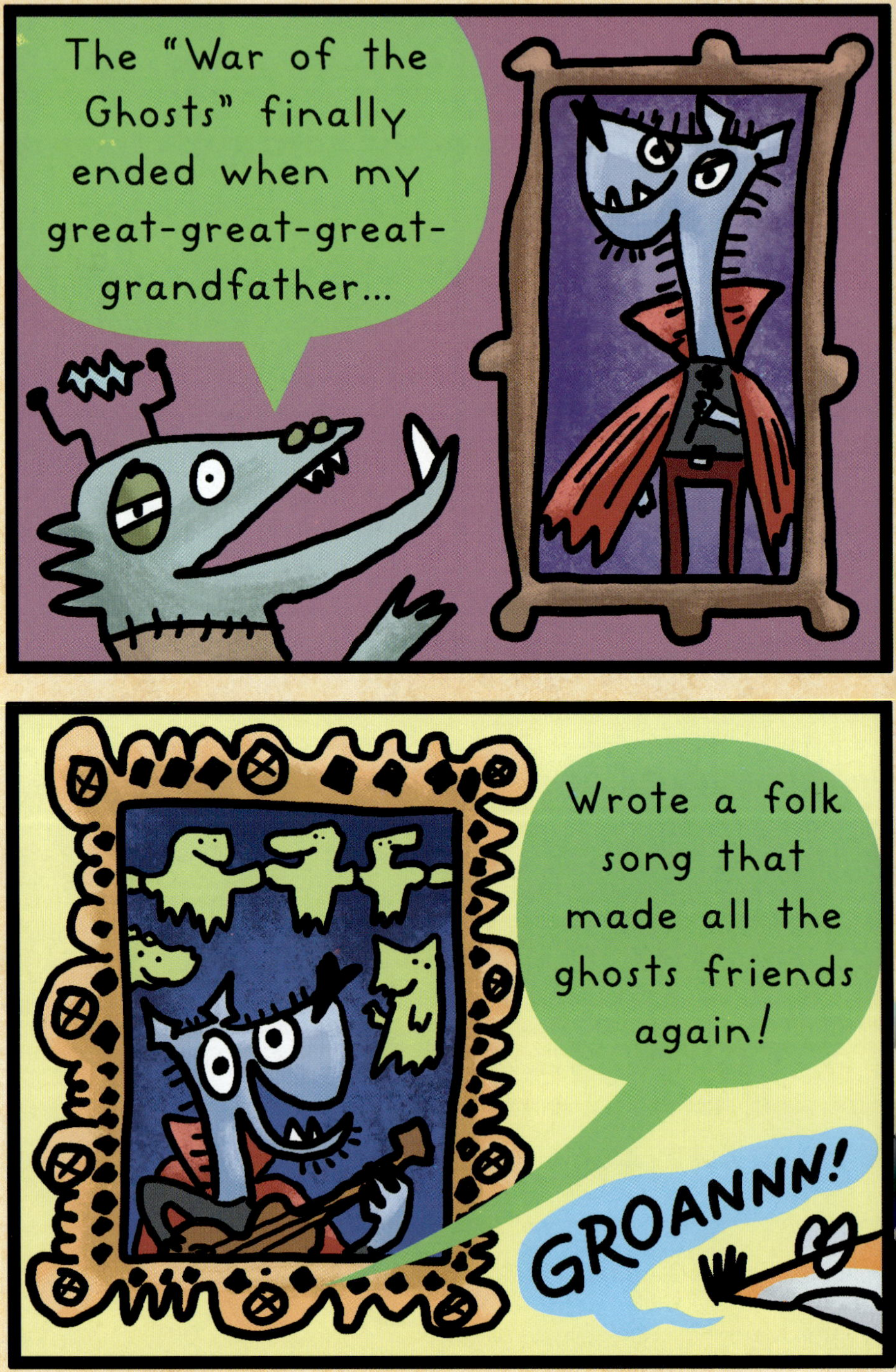

The "War of the Ghosts" finally ended when my great-great-great-grandfather...

Wrote a folk song that made all the ghosts friends again!

GROANNN!

The ghosts were so grateful that they made a solid gold coffin for him as a thank-you gift...

Somehow, over the years, the coffin was lost!

Until, in 1978, I found it in an antique store while shopping for

DISCO BOOTS!

I bought the coffin (and the boots), and thus was the gold coffin returned to Cacklefur Castle!

WHEE!

Ever since then, the golden coffin has been Cacklefur Castle's greatest treasure.

(The boots are a close second.)

Until tonight, when the coffin was "stolen."

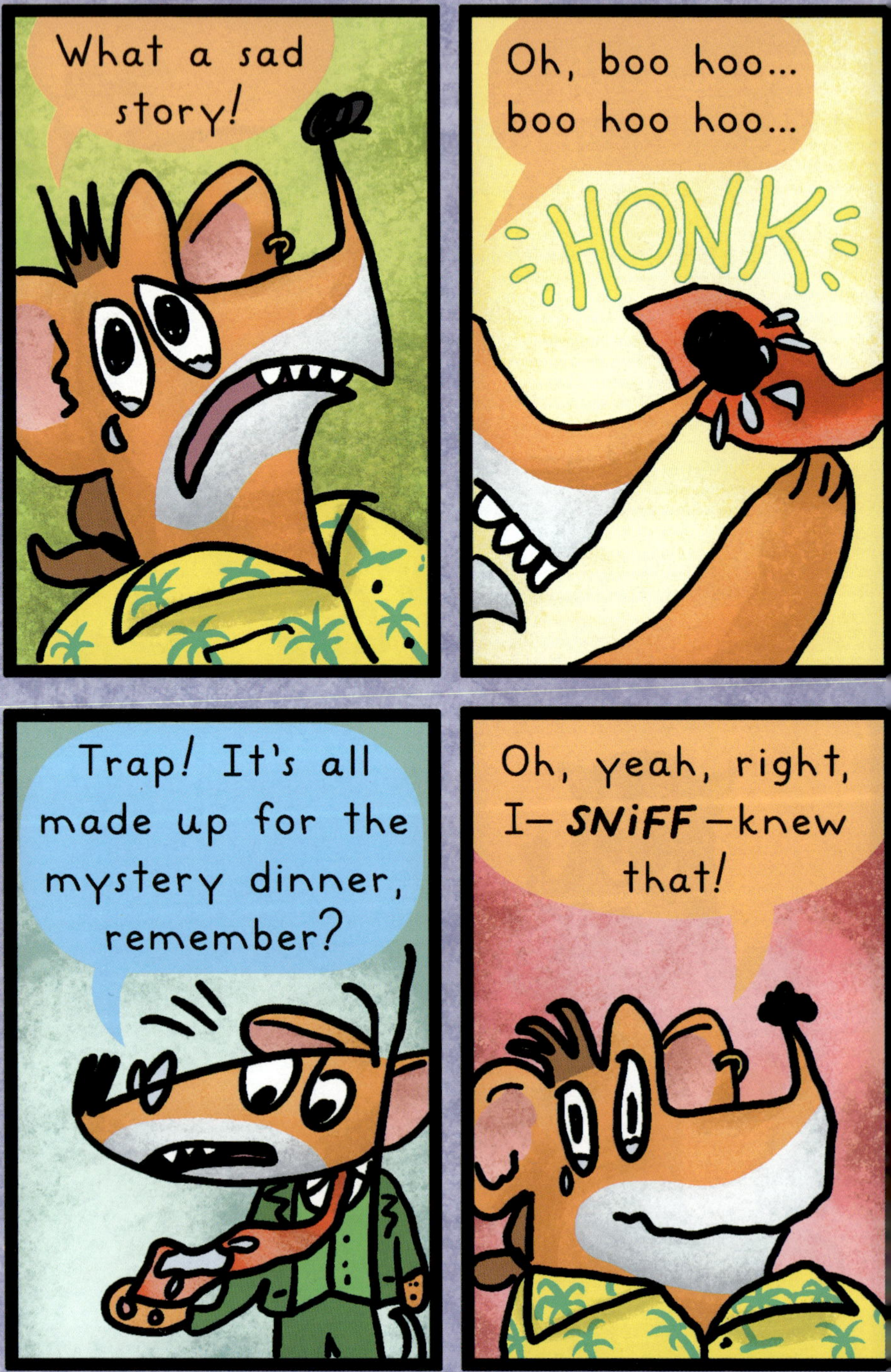

Trap! It's all made up for the mystery dinner, remember?

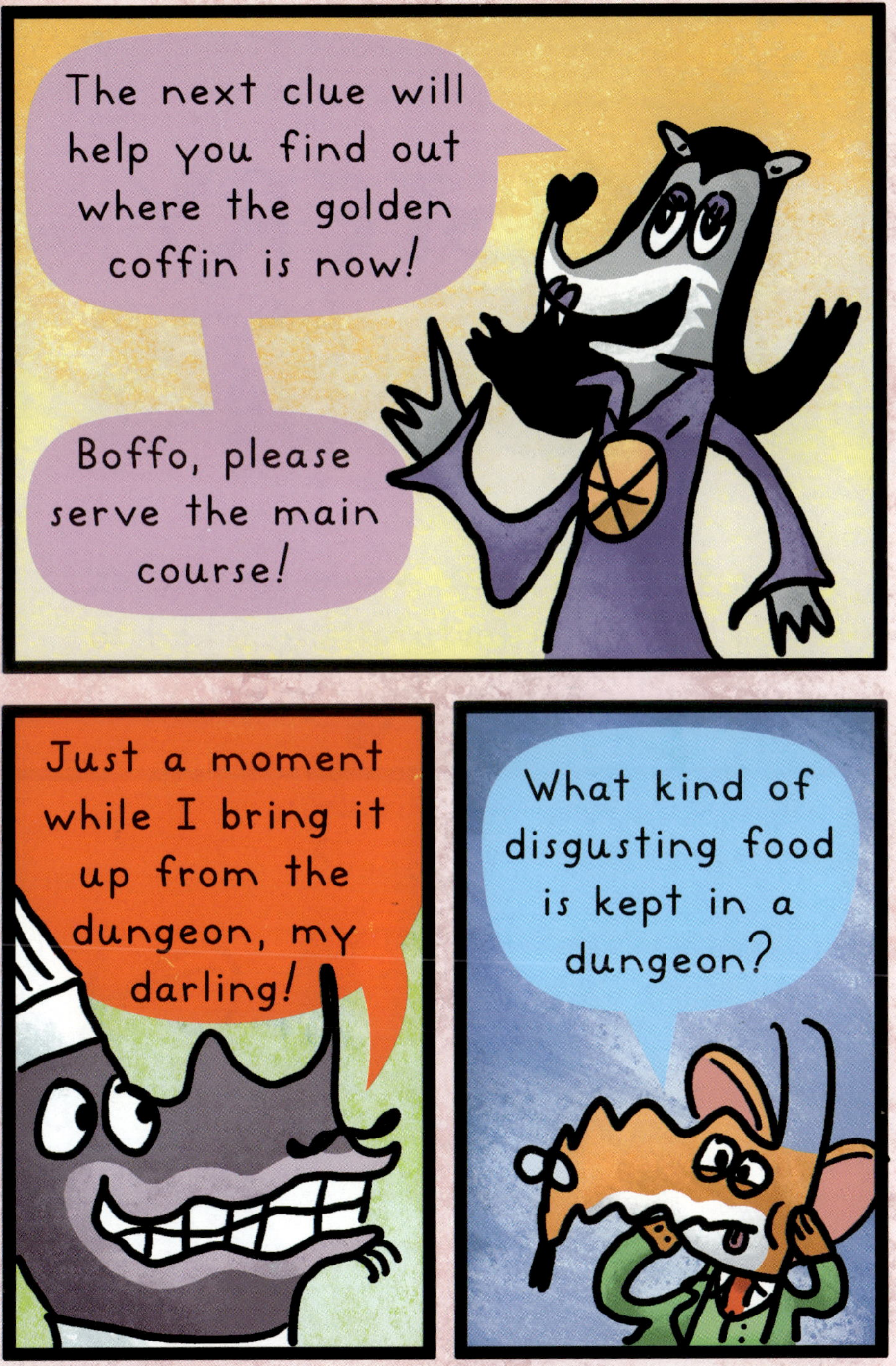

The next clue will help you find out where the golden coffin is now!

Boffo, please serve the main course!

CHAPTER FIFTEEN

MYSTERY GIBLETS

We took our seats while we waited for Boffo. Unfortunately, I had to sit next to *Rattata*.

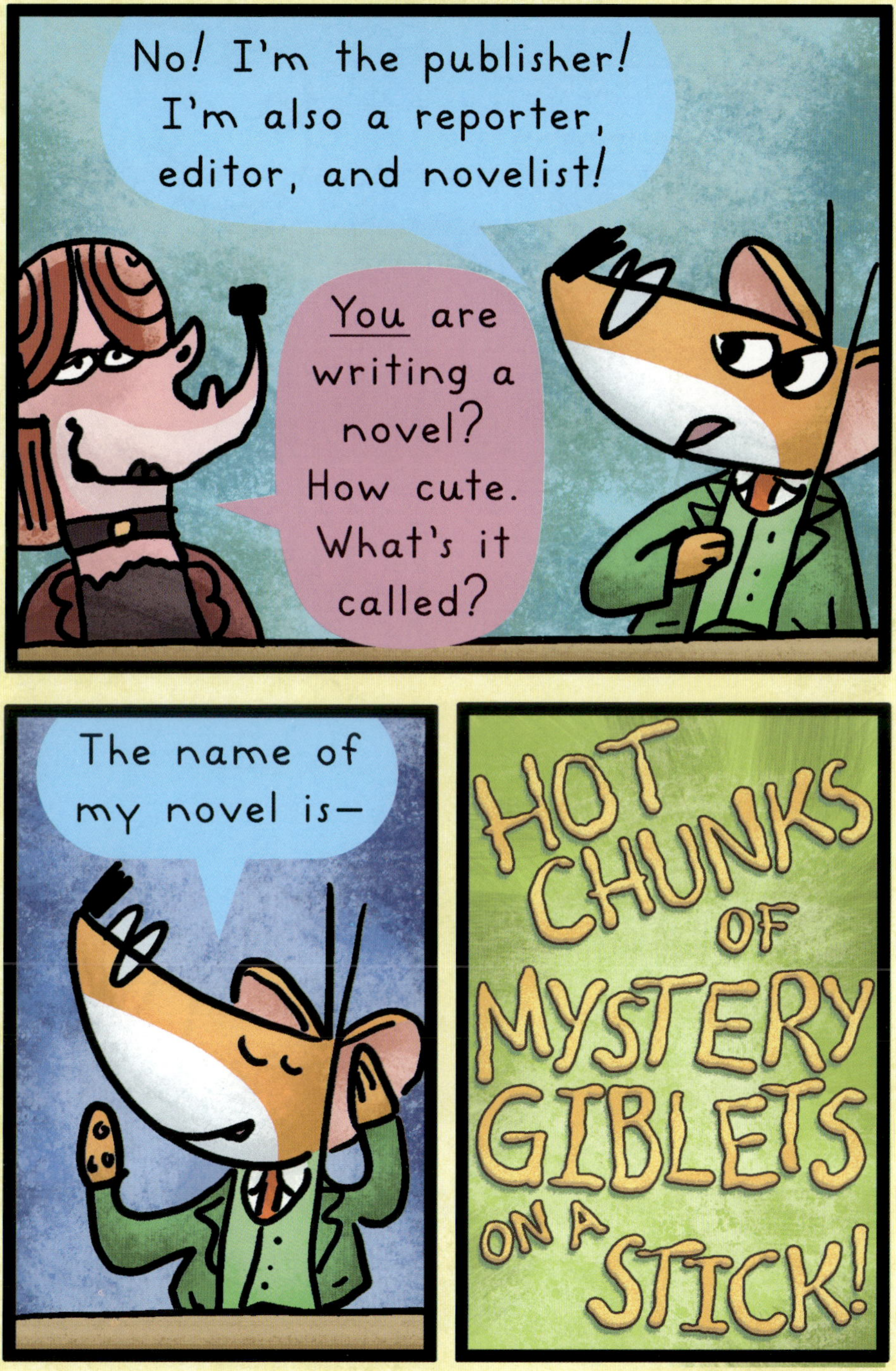

No! I'm the publisher! I'm also a reporter, editor, and novelist!

You are writing a novel? How cute. What's it called?

NO! That's not the name of my novel!

It's what Boffo had dragged out of the dungeon!

It was hot. And it was on a stick. But if it was a clue, I couldn't figure it out!

Trap ate his in one gulp!

Was there a clue inside of that?

If there was, it sure was YUMMY!

Pssst... Thea...
was there a
clue in yours?

I don't know. It
was so gross I
fed it to the
GIANT ROACH
under the table.

There's a giant
roach under the
table?!?!?

Not anymore.
After one bite,
it went home
sick...

Why me? How did a Nice mouse like me end up with a POCKET full of HOT giblets— which are probably covered in cockroach slobber — while stuck in a CASTLE with WEREWOLF SLUGS on the night of a FULL MOON???

To escape, I had to solve the mystery! To do that, I had to get the next clue! To do that, I had to...

NIBBLE

SPLURT!

MY MOUTH IS ON FIRE!

How do you like the "hot chunks"? Filled with the hottest sauce on Mouse Island!

TRANSRATANIA REAPER SAUCE!

In the name of pepper jack*, somebody give me a drink!

*Pepper jack is a kind of spicy cheese.

MOAT SLIME

I give up! I can't find the next clue!

MOAT SLIME

Oh, sorry!

I forgot to mention...

This clue isn't in the food. It's in the entertainment!

Ready or not... here I come!

Suddenly, Creepella's father, Baron Boris Von Cacklefur, ran in...

Good evening, rodents! I'd like to welcome you to a "bury" special night at the castle! Ha! Ha! Ha!

Was that you BOOing, or was it the castle ghosts? Ha! Ha! Ha! But seriously, folks...

This is a GRAVE matter... You could DIE laughing! Can you DIG it?

Boris's jokes were too CORNY, too CREEPY, and way too LONG.

So then the zombie says to the ghoul, "Musicals? I thought you said mouse skulls?" And the ghoul says, "I did, it's called *Mouse Skulls: The Musical.*" So the zombie says, "How much do tickets cost?" and the other ghoul says, "The price is your immortal soul, or twelve bucks if it's a matinee." "I can't come to the matinee," said the zombie. "Why not?" said the ghoul. So the zombie says... "I'm dating a vampire." Ha ha ha! Get it? Because vampires only come out at night and matinees are in the afternoon? Get it? Hilarious, huh? Ha ha ha! Okay, stop me if you've heard this one, a squid and a snallyghaster crawl into a graveyard...

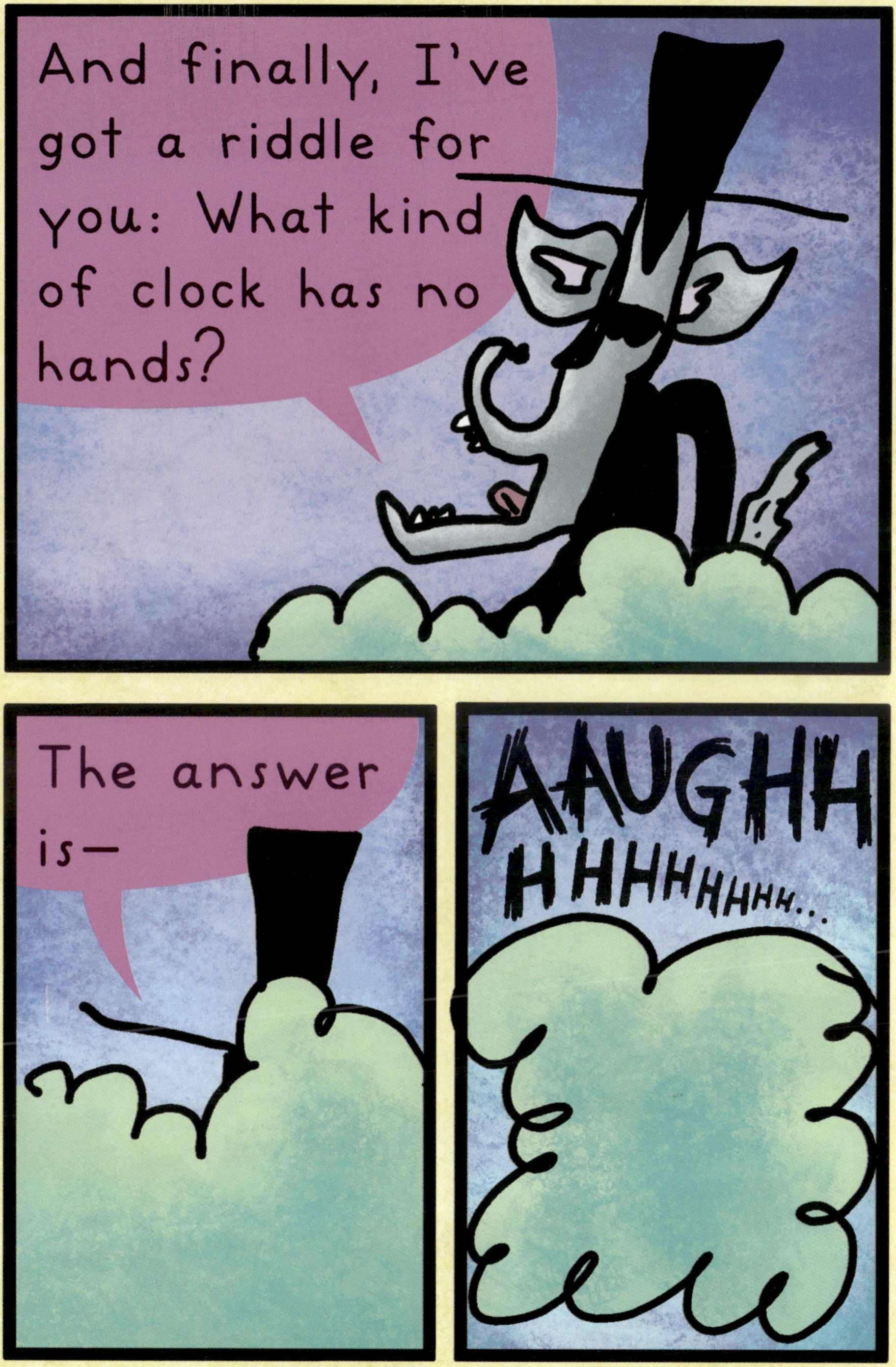

And finally, I've got a riddle for you: What kind of clock has no hands?

P.U., Gerry, you should at least say "excuse me"!

But...
...I didn't...
It wasn't...
...I never...
Not me!

It's okay, Gerrykins!
That was just Daddy's final joke!

So... can you solve the riddle he left? It's the next clue!
WHAT KIND OF CLOCK HAS NO HANDS?

CHAPTER SEVENTEEN

IT'S GETTING LATE!

Everybody tried guessing the answer to the riddle...

Ten o'clock?

RANCID RICOTTA!

Thea, solve the mystery so we can get outta here!

A clock with no hands is a sundial!

Sundials use shadows to point to the correct time.

Earlier, I noticed one in the castle garden. I bet the next clue is there!

Well done, Thea! Follow me to the garden, everyone!

CHAPTER EIGHTEEN

GO AHEAD, SCAREDY-MOUSE!

We followed Creepella through about a mile of creepy halls and secret passages to the garden.

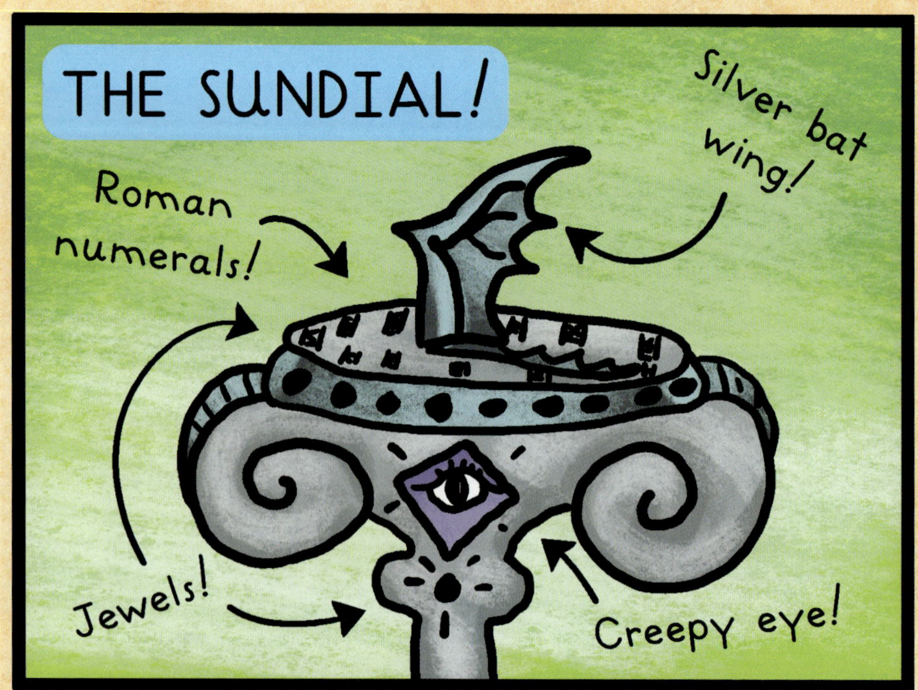

The moondial is pointing at that crack in the wall...

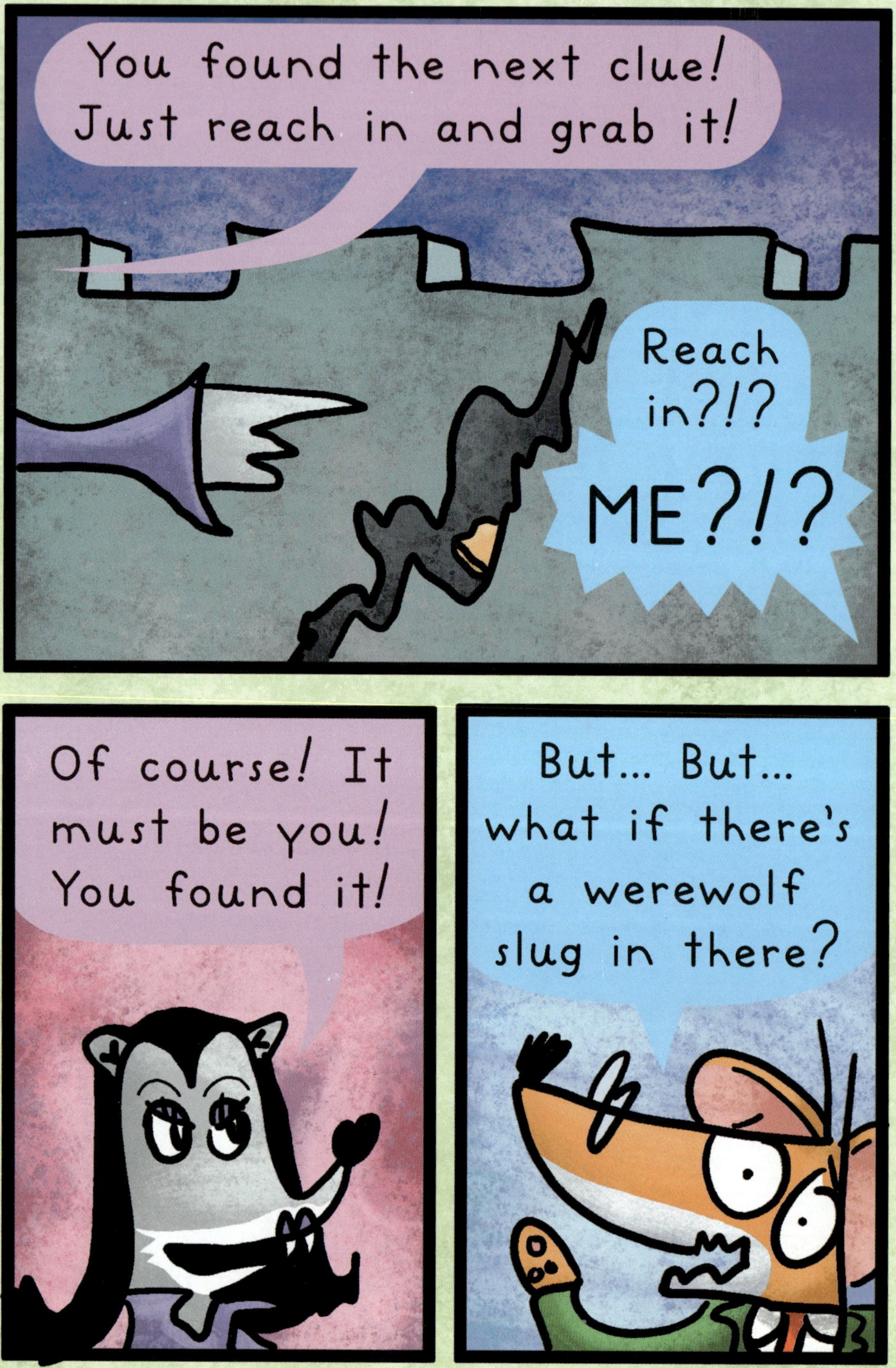

You found the next clue! Just reach in and grab it!

Reach in?!?

ME?!?

Don't be silly!
Snip + Snap put
the slugs away.
Right, boys?

I closed my eyes, reaching into the creepy crevice, and felt something cold and metal...

I pulled out the ugliest bell in the world!

CHAPTER NINETEEN

THE Sweet, Sad Song OF THE WERE CANARY

A **HORRIFYING** bird-thing swooped out of the dark!!

PUTRID PARMESAN!*

IT'S ON MY HEAD!

*Parmesan is a type of... Oh, never mind!

Relax! Caruso lives in the hair of our housekeeper, **MADAME LATOMB.** They will now sing the next clue...

Normal canaries go
TWEET + CHEEP,
My WERECANARY
will make you WEEP!

GLOOM GLOOM

Guests of the castle, ye are a'failin'
And that has set my bird a'wailin'!

WAIL WAIL

The coffin is lost. Cannot be found!
And all you did was goof around!

GLOOM GLOOM

My canary's song is full of woe
Because all of you are so slow!

WOE! WOE!

While you ate, it grew late!
And soon the clock will tell your fate!

DOOM! DOOM!

It's so...
so... SAD!

Oh, boo-hoo!
So sad!
Sniff
We'll never solve it!
Woe!
Hold me!
WAH!
And never win Creepella's heart!
My heart... breaking!
Alas!
I am also deeply moved.

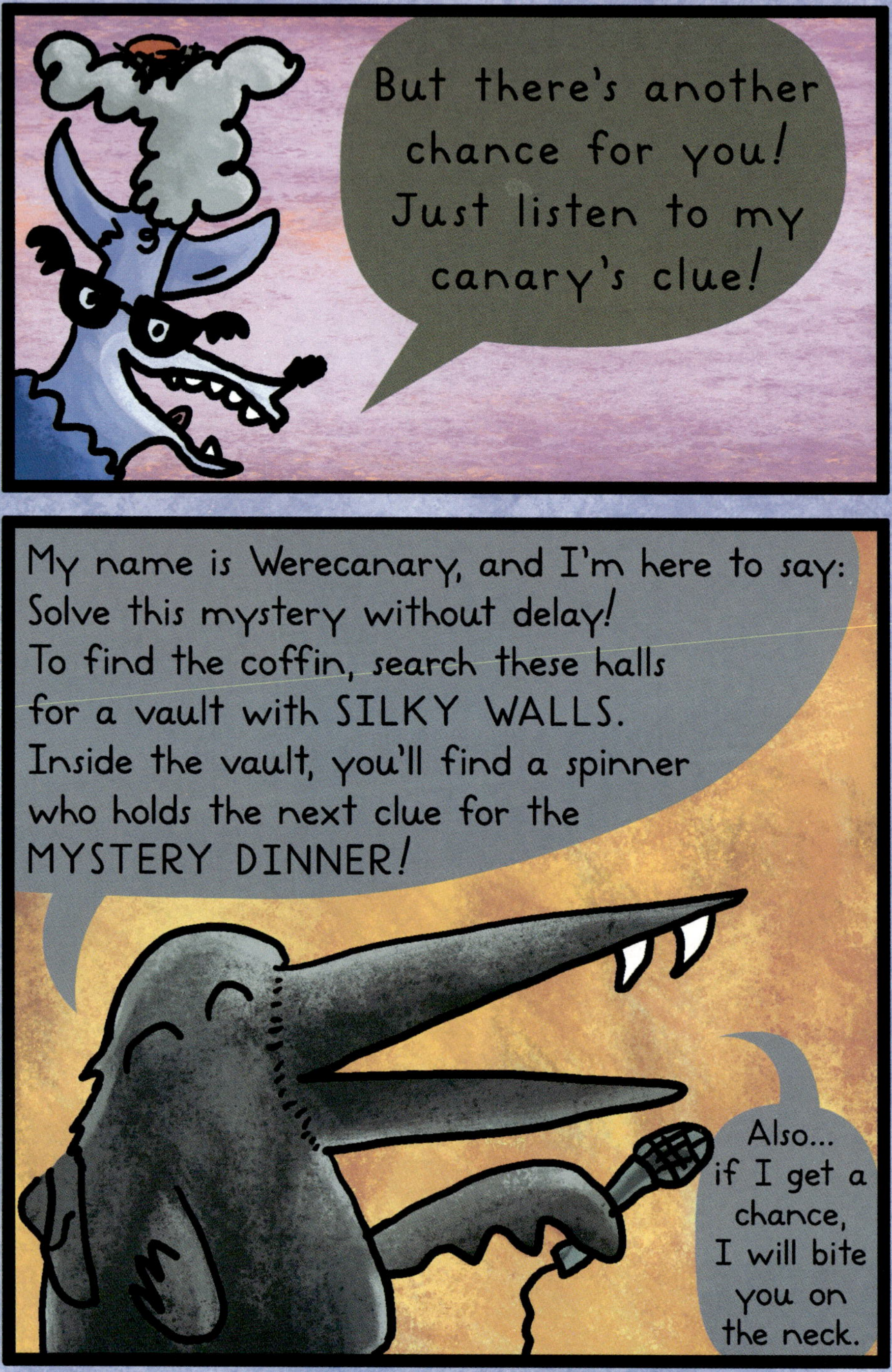

My name is Werecanary, and I'm here to say:
Solve this mystery without delay!
To find the coffin, search these halls
for a vault with SILKY WALLS.
Inside the vault, you'll find a spinner
who holds the next clue for the
MYSTERY DINNER!

Also... if I get a chance, I will bite you on the neck.

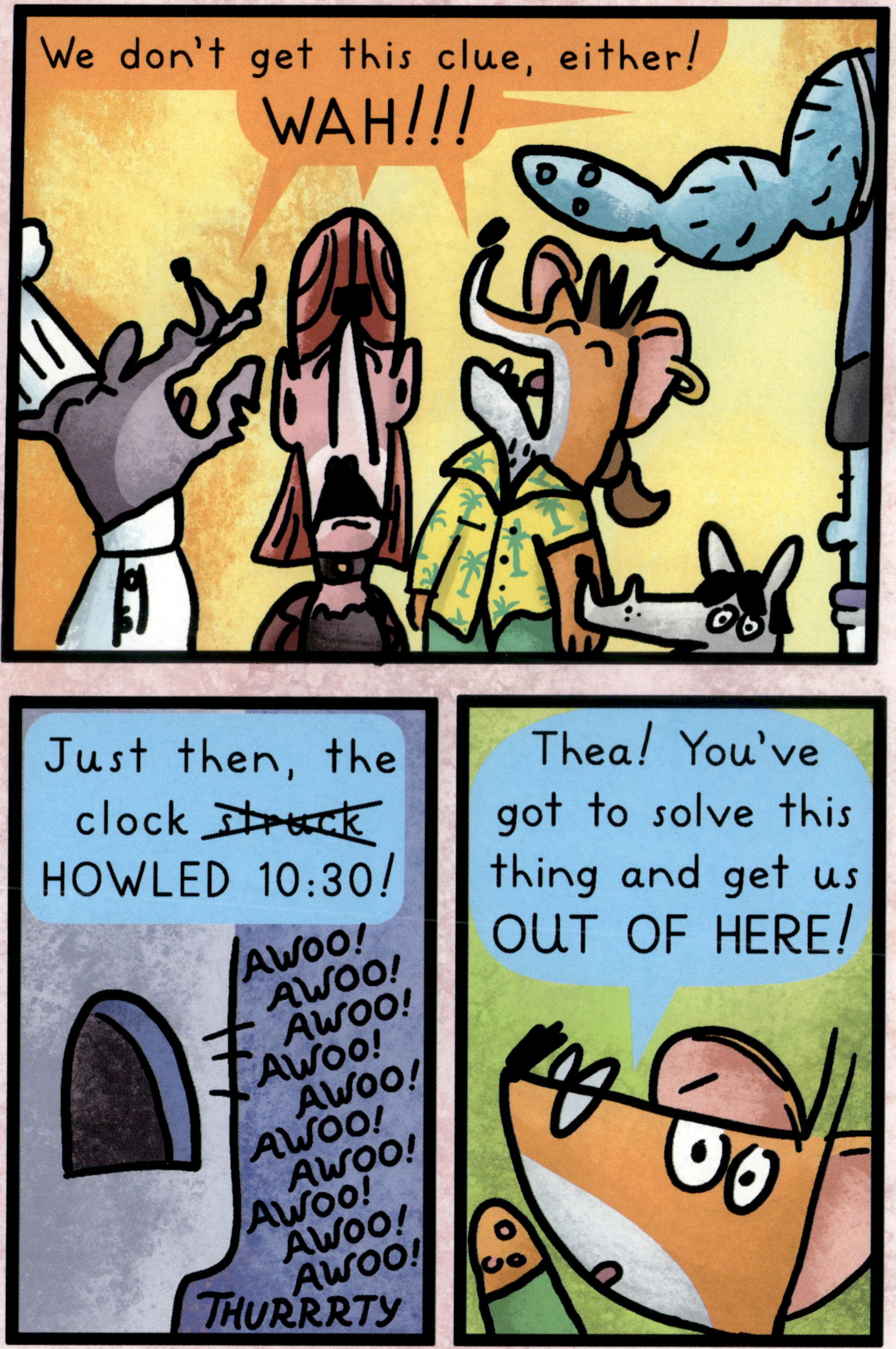

We don't get this clue, either!
WAH!!!

As Creepella led us back to the dining room, Thea told me:

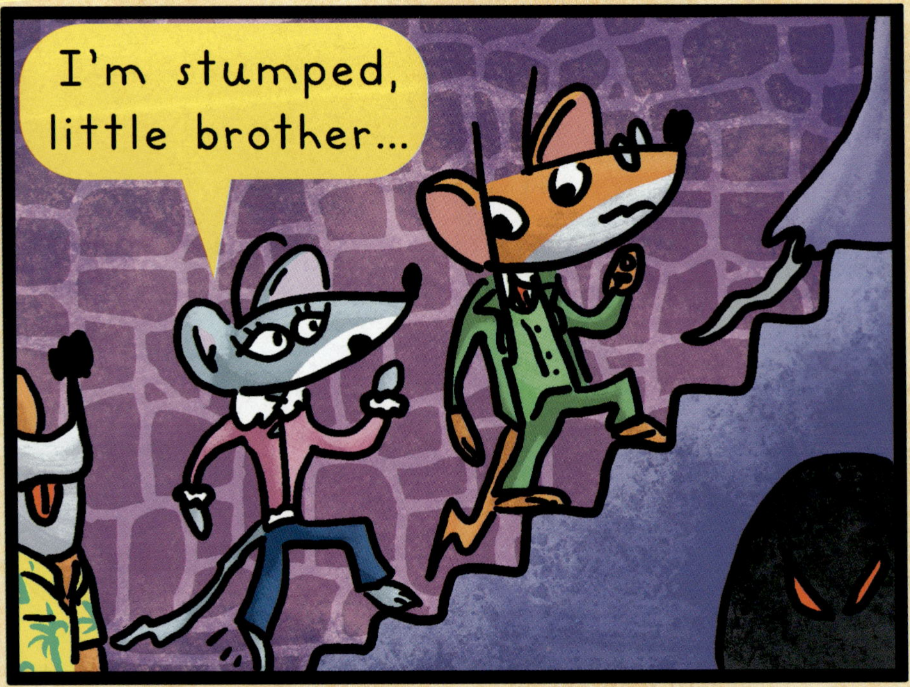

I'm stumped, little brother...

The clue clearly points to Lady Silken-Smythe, the spider. But I don't know where she is.

I do! She ran through that door after she bit me!

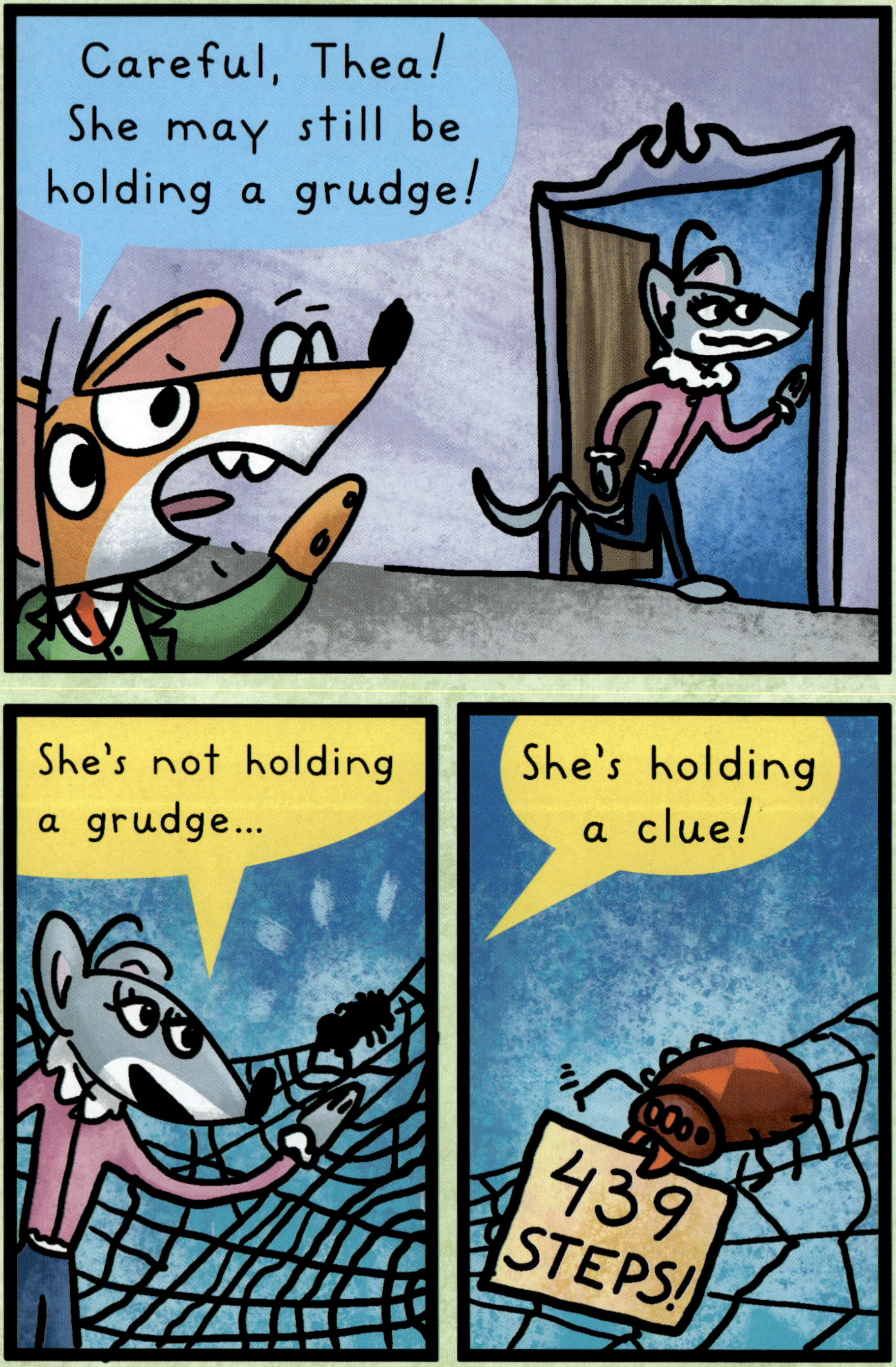

Careful, Thea! She may still be holding a grudge!

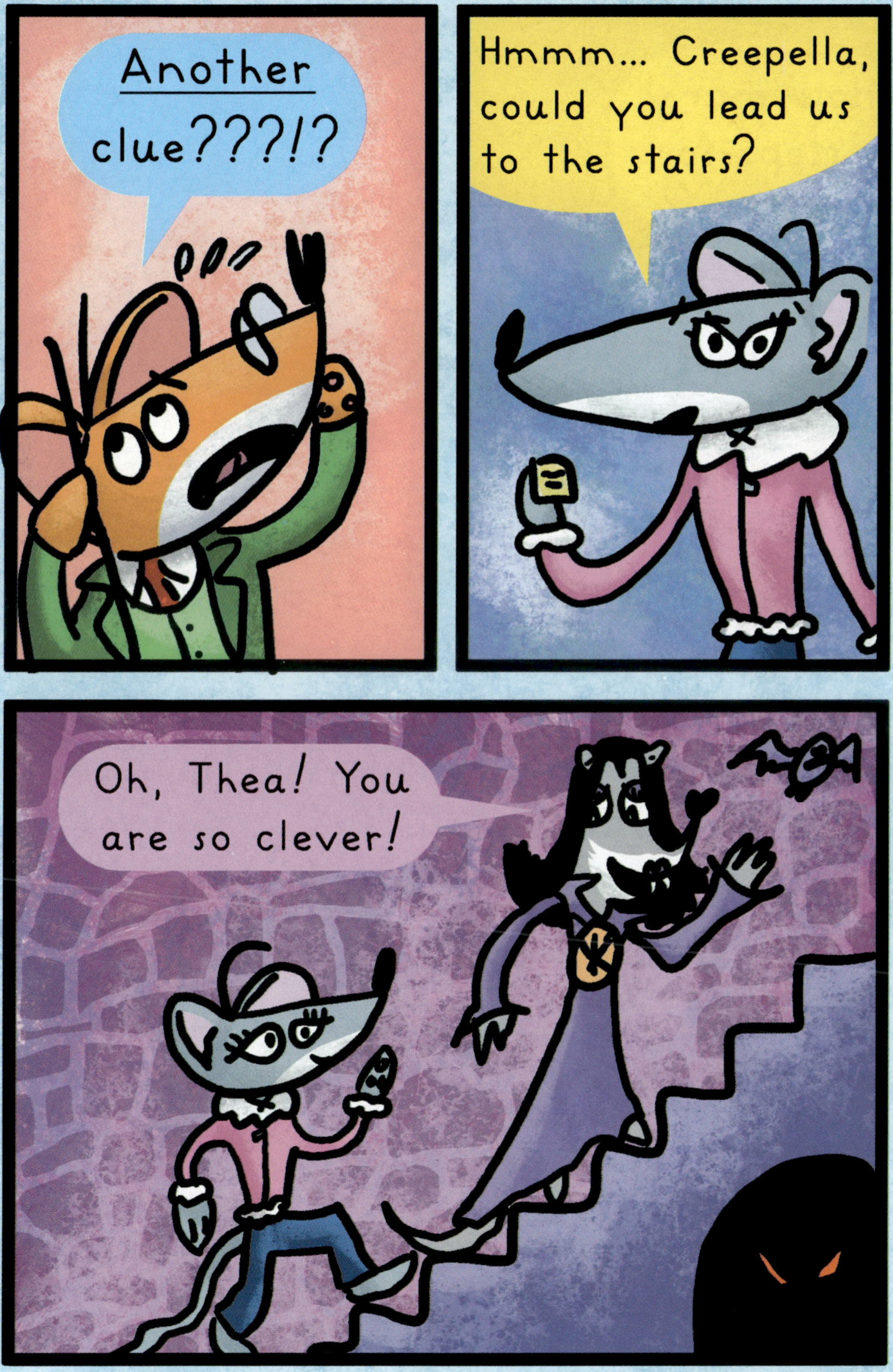

Oh, Thea! You are so clever!

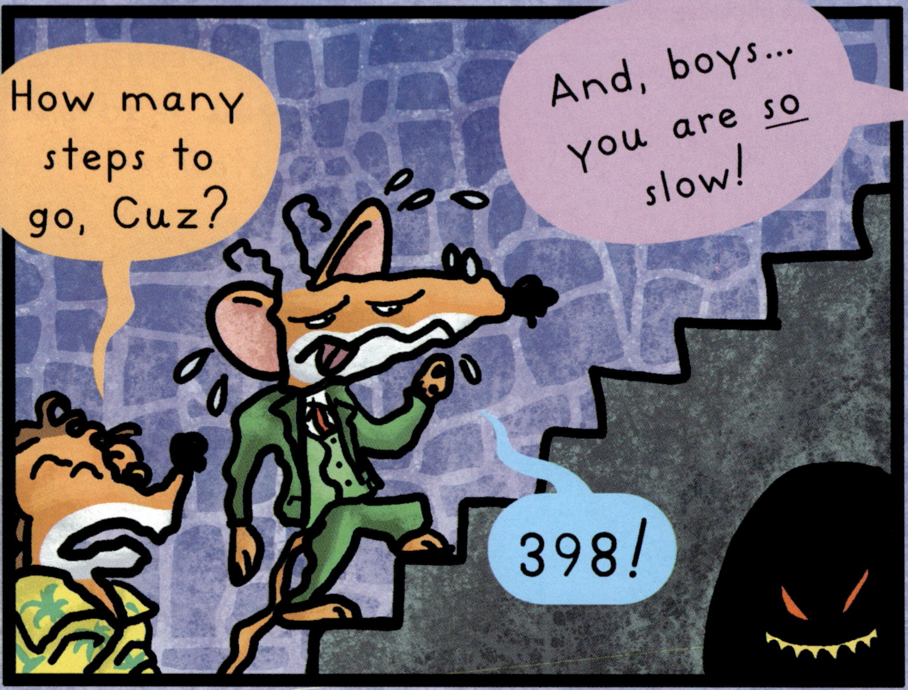

How many steps to go, Cuz?

And, boys... you are so slow!

398!

The steps went all the way up to the castle's tallest tower. By the time we got there, Thea had already found the next clue...

To the dungeon!
This is the dungeon? 
There was a wallpaper mix-up...
Here's the clue... "Check this out!"

TO THE LIBRARY!

TO THE MOAT!

To the music room!

To the attic!

To grandpa's disco boot closet!

To the third door on the right!

Then, as we were running past the dining room, we heard:

AWOO! AWOO! AWOO!
AWOO! AWOO! AWOO!
AWOO! AWOO! AWOO!
AWOOOO! AWOOOOO!

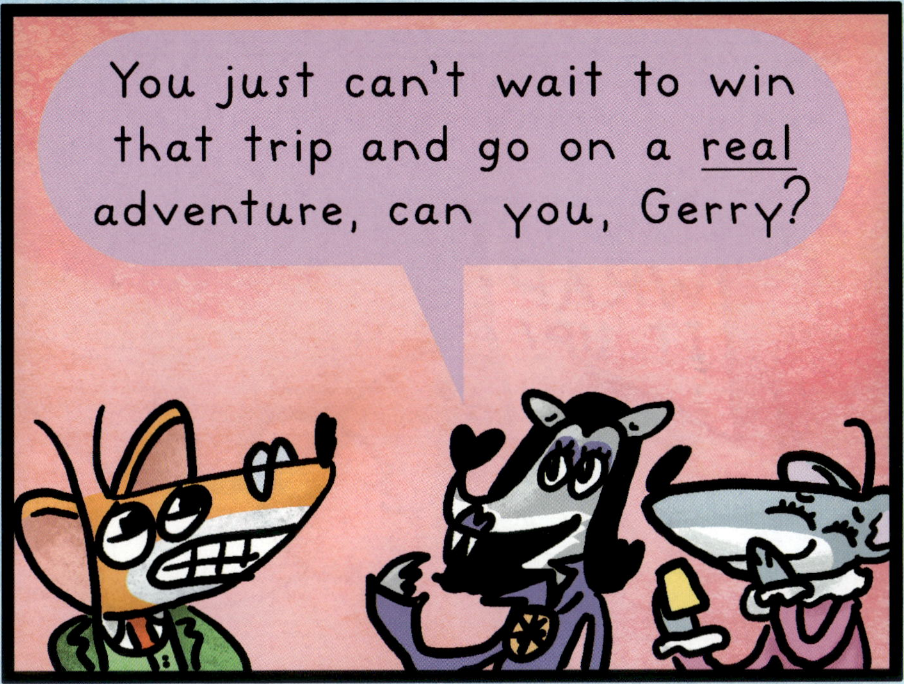

You just can't wait to win that trip and go on a real adventure, can you, Gerry?

That trip was the last thing I wanted! The first thing I wanted was to get out of there before **MIDNIGHT!** But, I always try to be a polite mouse.

Well, don't worry! I promise Thea is holding the last clue!

TIME TO WRAP IT UP!

Wrapping up a burrito?

Wrapping up a knee injury?

Wrapping up a book's plot?

Rapping?

Wrapping a gag gift!

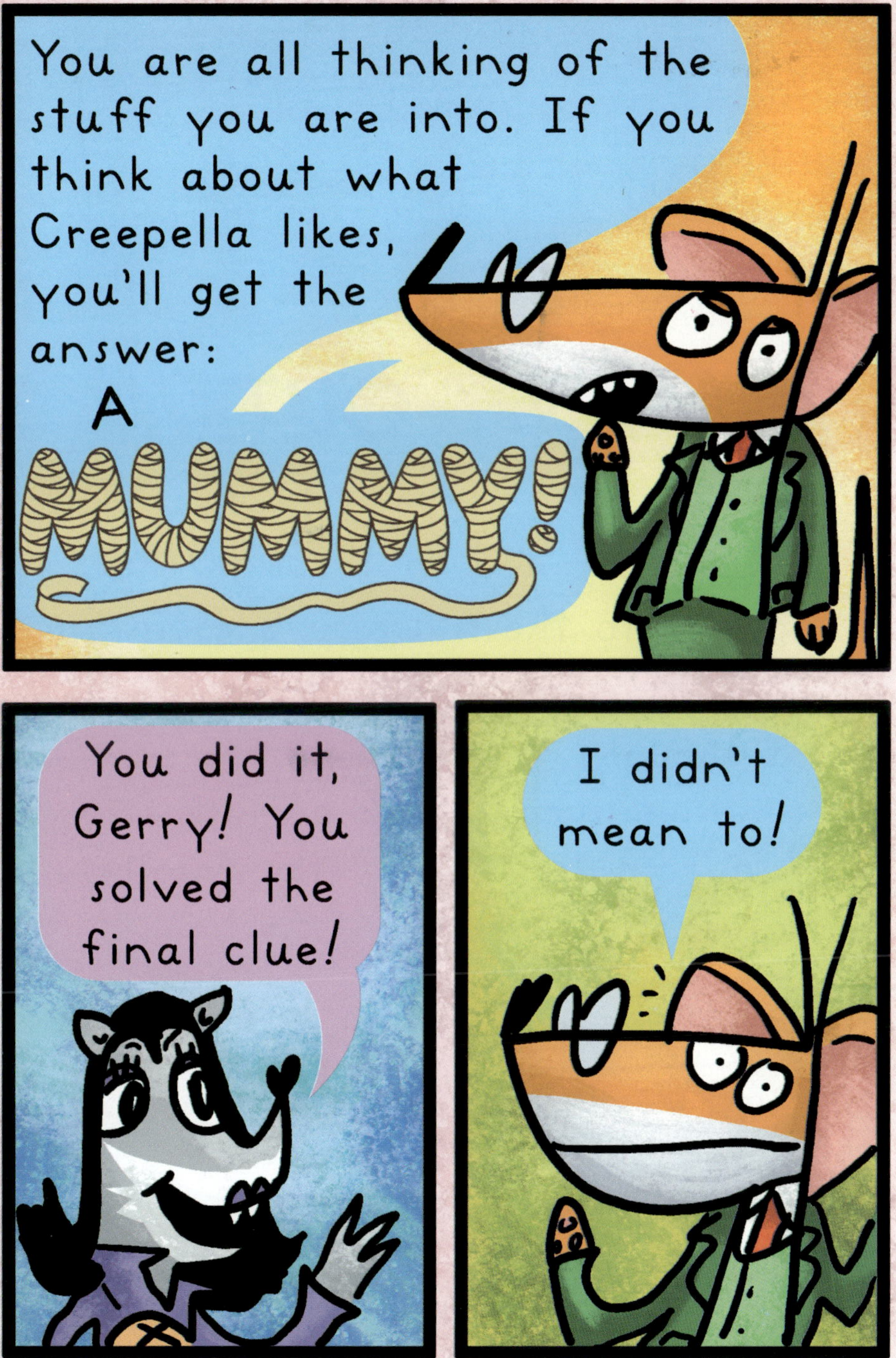

You are all thinking of the stuff you are into. If you think about what Creepella likes, you'll get the answer:

A MUMMY!

CHAPTER TWENTY-ONE

SUDDENLY, THE LIGHTS WENT OUT!!!

Creepella led us through the castle to the mummy's room...

As we were passing the kitchen, Boffo spoke up...

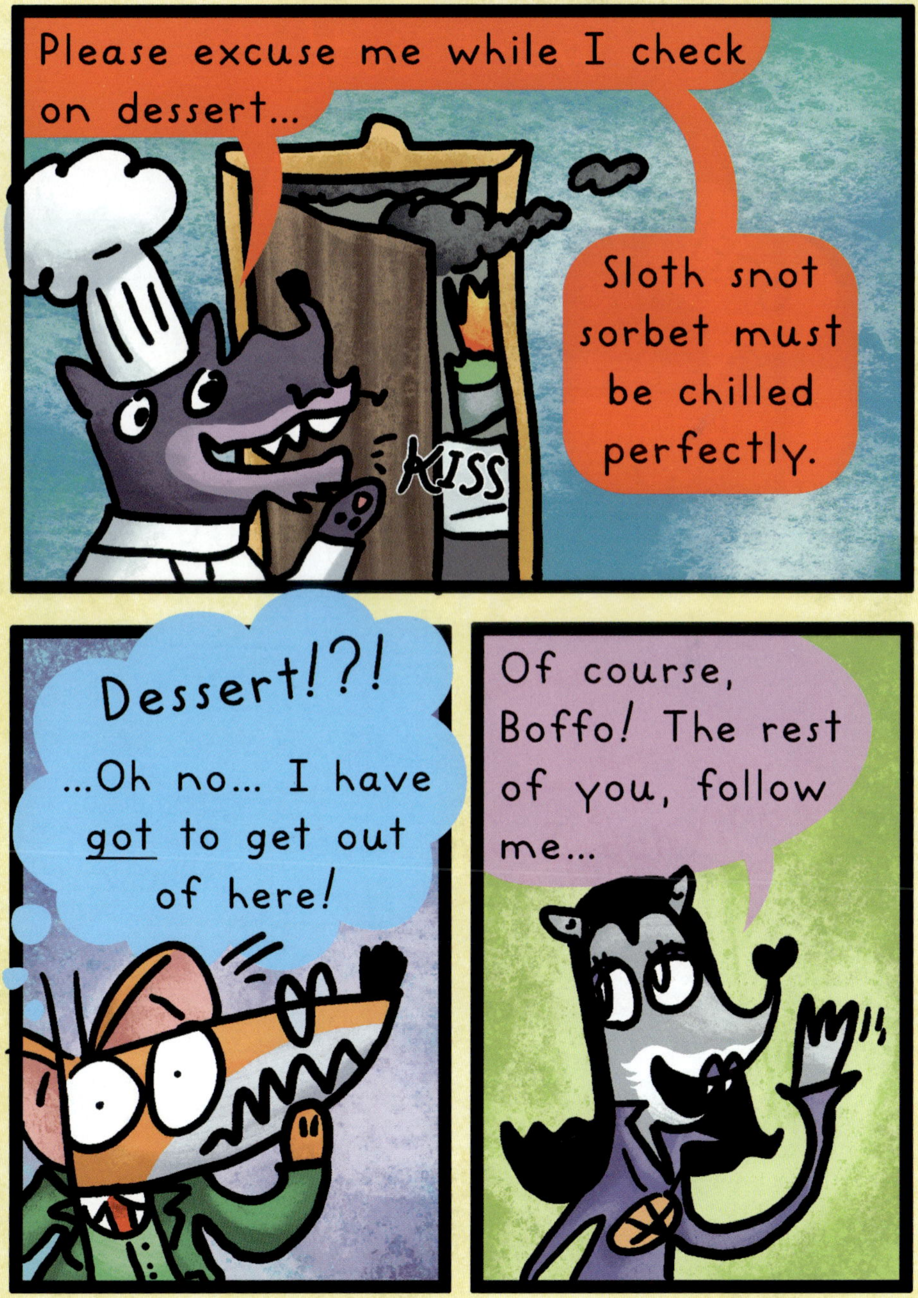

Please excuse me while I check on dessert...

KISS

Sloth snot sorbet must be chilled perfectly.

Suddenly, the lights went out!

Trap somehow stepped on my tail thirteen times before Creepella lit a candle...

I have to admit, the lights going out was a nice, **CREEPY** touch, Creepella!

But... I didn't plan this! And now I'm getting creeped out!

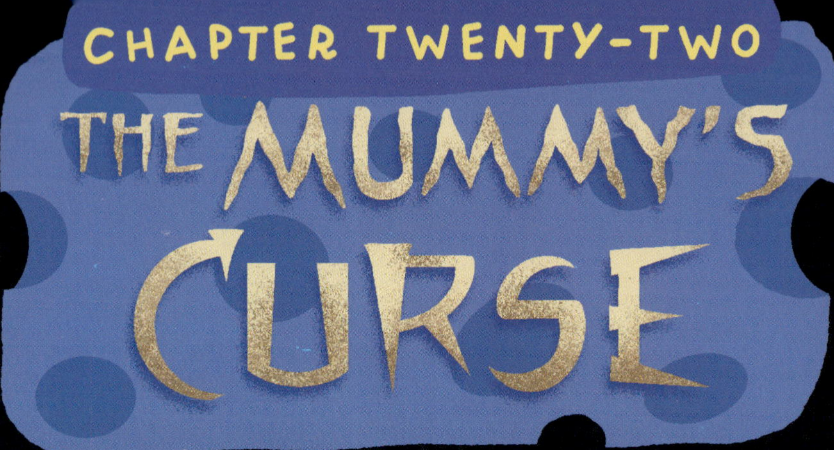

Creepella was still trying to explain that she didn't know why the lights were off, when...

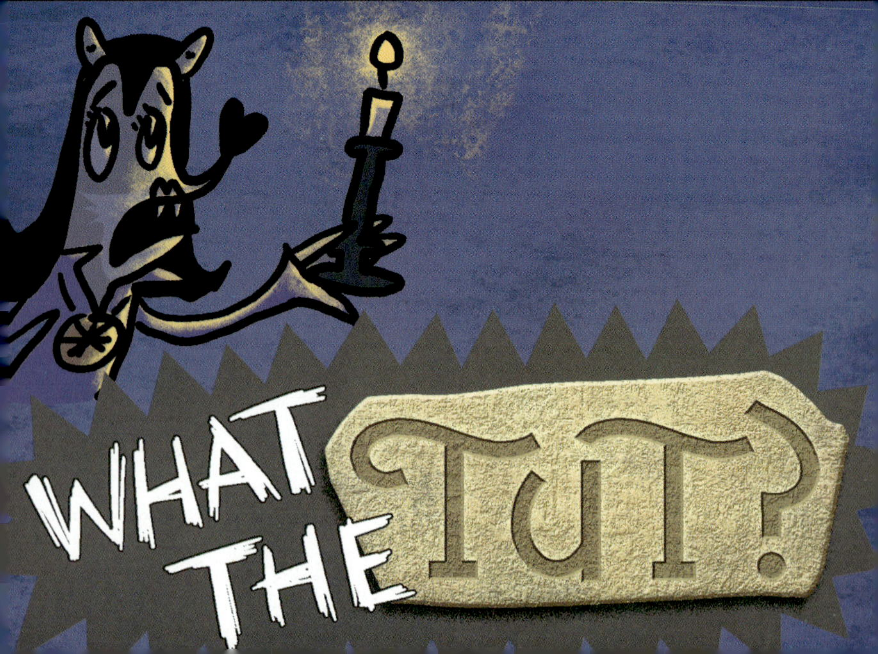

WHAT THE TUT?

BLUE CHEESE CRUMBLES!
Who was that?
It was the mummy! Quick, let's get to her room!

Grandpa and I were playing MICECRAFT ... then the lights went out.

By the time I lit a candle, the golden coffin was GONE!

Wait... we're confused!

Stolen as part of the mystery game or...

REALLY STOLEN!

CHAPTER TWENTY-THREE

The Truth Is...

Snip + Snap, who had turned out the lights as a prank, turned them back on so we could look for the coffin.

This is all my fault!

Your fault, Grandpa? How?

I told a lie! I said the golden coffin was made of gold!

But...

...the truth is... it's just... really, really OLD CHEESE!

The coffin is priceless to our family, but WORTHLESS to anyone else...

But one of you must have believed it was real gold...

SO YOU STOLE IT!

HISSSS!

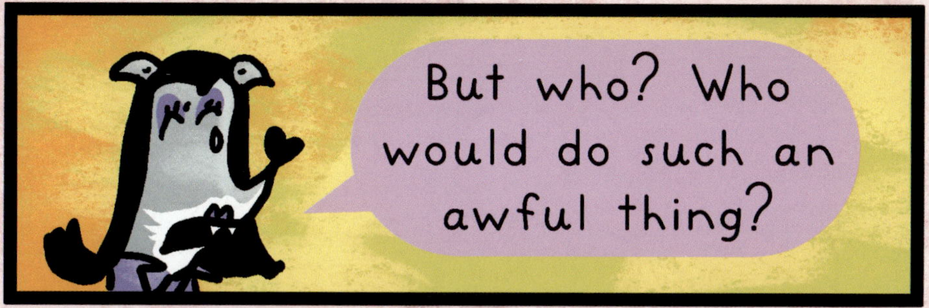

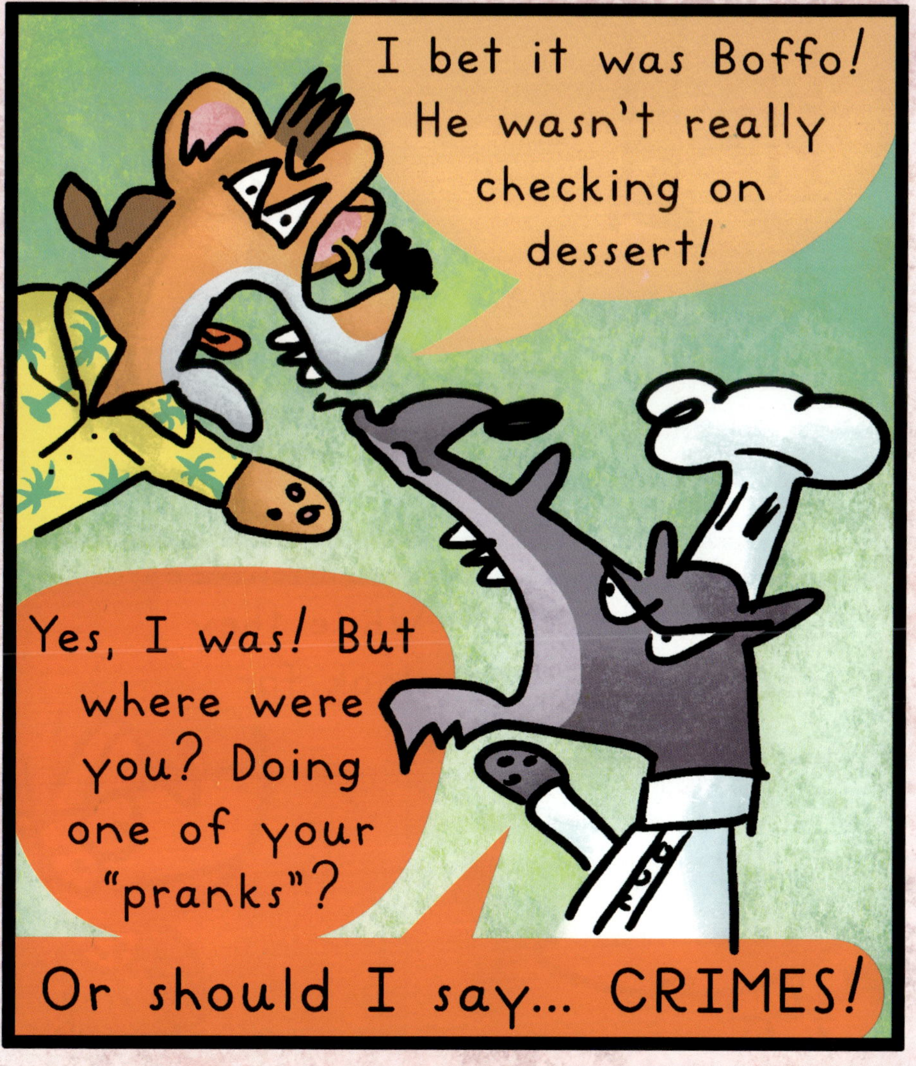

I bet it was Boffo! He wasn't really checking on dessert!

Yes, I was! But where were you? Doing one of your "pranks"?

Or should I say... CRIMES!

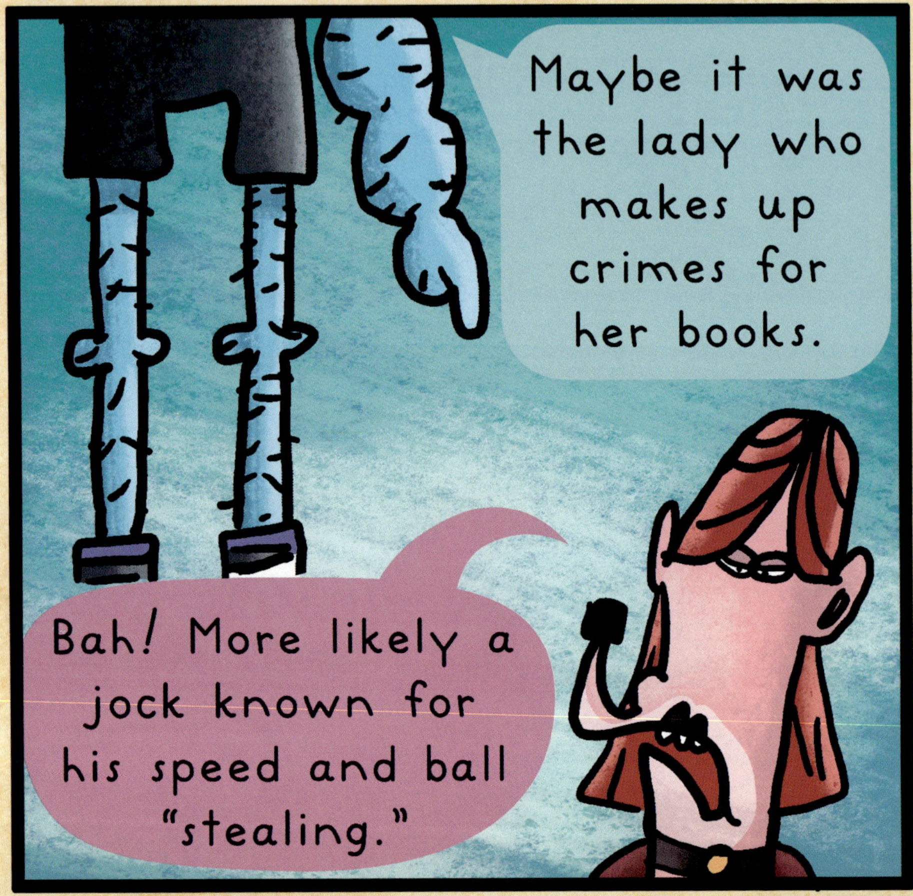

Maybe it was the lady who makes up crimes for her books.

Bah! More likely a jock known for his speed and ball "stealing."

CHAPTER TWENTY-FOUR

A SLIMY DISCOVERY

Thea and I examined the scene of the slime—I mean, crime!

Try to focus, Gerry Berry! We're looking for a clue!

Well, there's nothing here but socks, stink, and dessert!

Dessert?
Yeah, there's PUTRID purple slime all over. Boffo probably wants us to eat it for—

That's not dessert! That's a slime trail leading right out the door!!!

You think our dessert snuck out the door?

No, **BRIE* BRAIN!** The THIEF snuck out the door!

*Brie is a kind of cheese. "Brie brain" is not a nice thing to call your brother!

Hey!

Sorry, Gerry Berry! I'm just in a hurry to...

FOLLOW THAT SLIME!

It goes across
the floor and
out the door

Down the stairs
and under
some
chairs

Across the hall and...

Have you noticed that everything rhymes?

This could be a book called

SLIME'S RHYMES!

Gerry! Hurry up!

CALDECATT

Now, let's see...

What rhymes with "across the hall"?

SMASH!

Into a wall?

CHAPTER TWENTY-FIVE

A ~~SECRET~~ SECRET PASSAGE!

After I recovered my senses, we ran back to get the others and show them what we found!

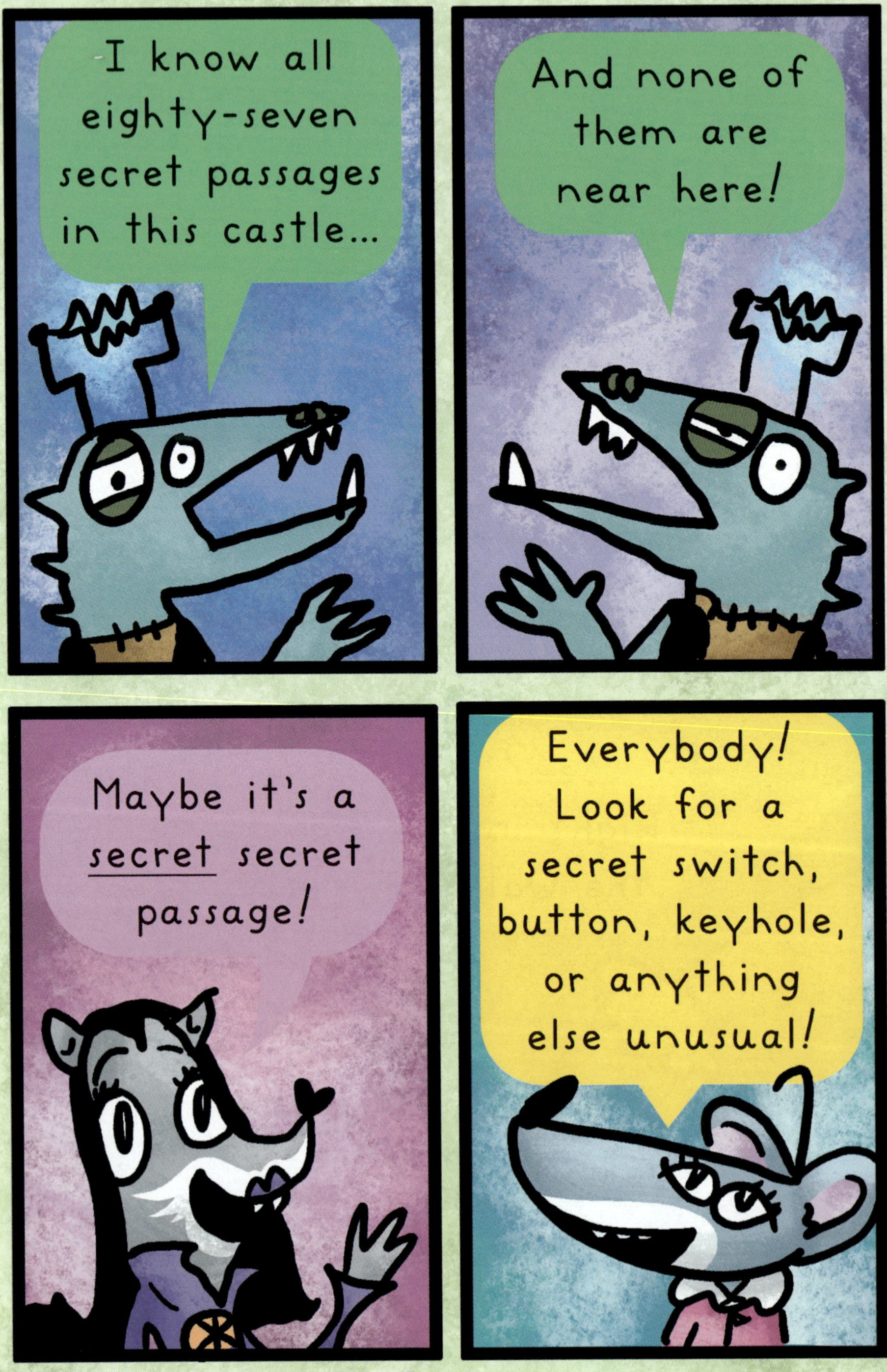

I know all
eighty-seven
secret passages
in this castle...

Hey, Thea! I found something unusual.

H'yuk! H'yuk!

Actually, we found several unusual things...

...but nothing that opened up a secret passage.

Maybe you're looking too low...

I see a button right here.

PUSH

We heard a RUMBLING ...

Part of the wall slid up...

Then the floor tilted, and we all tumbled into the secret passage.

Hall

Floor

Wall

Zombie foot

Slide

Us

*Queso blanco is a kind of cheese sauce.

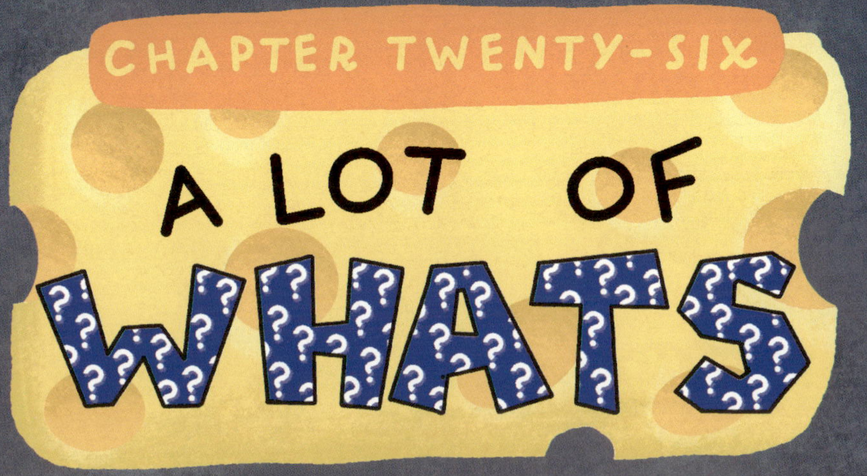

The slide ended in a cave flooded with slime!

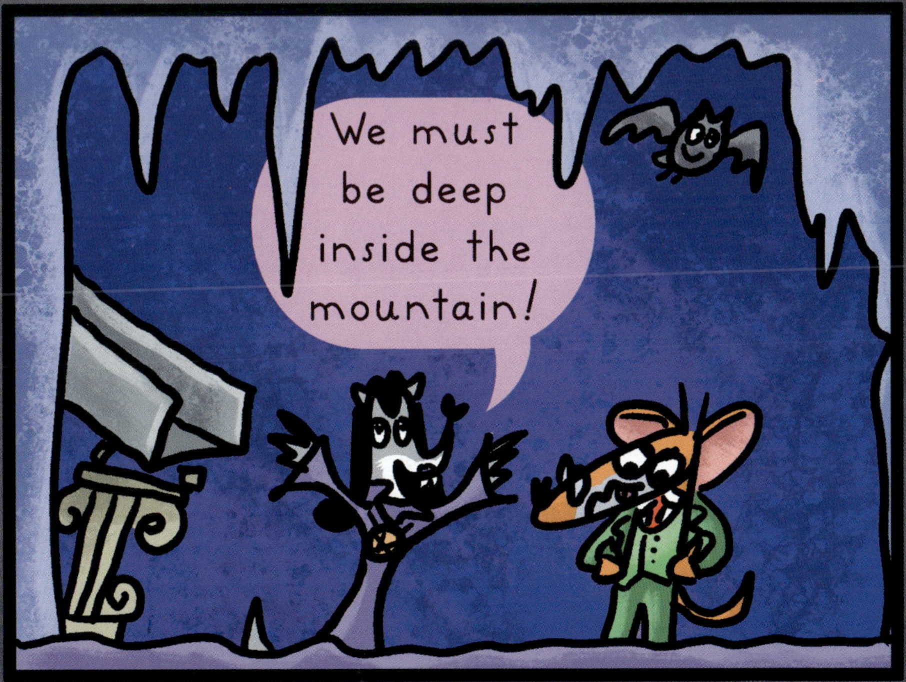

We must be deep inside the mountain!

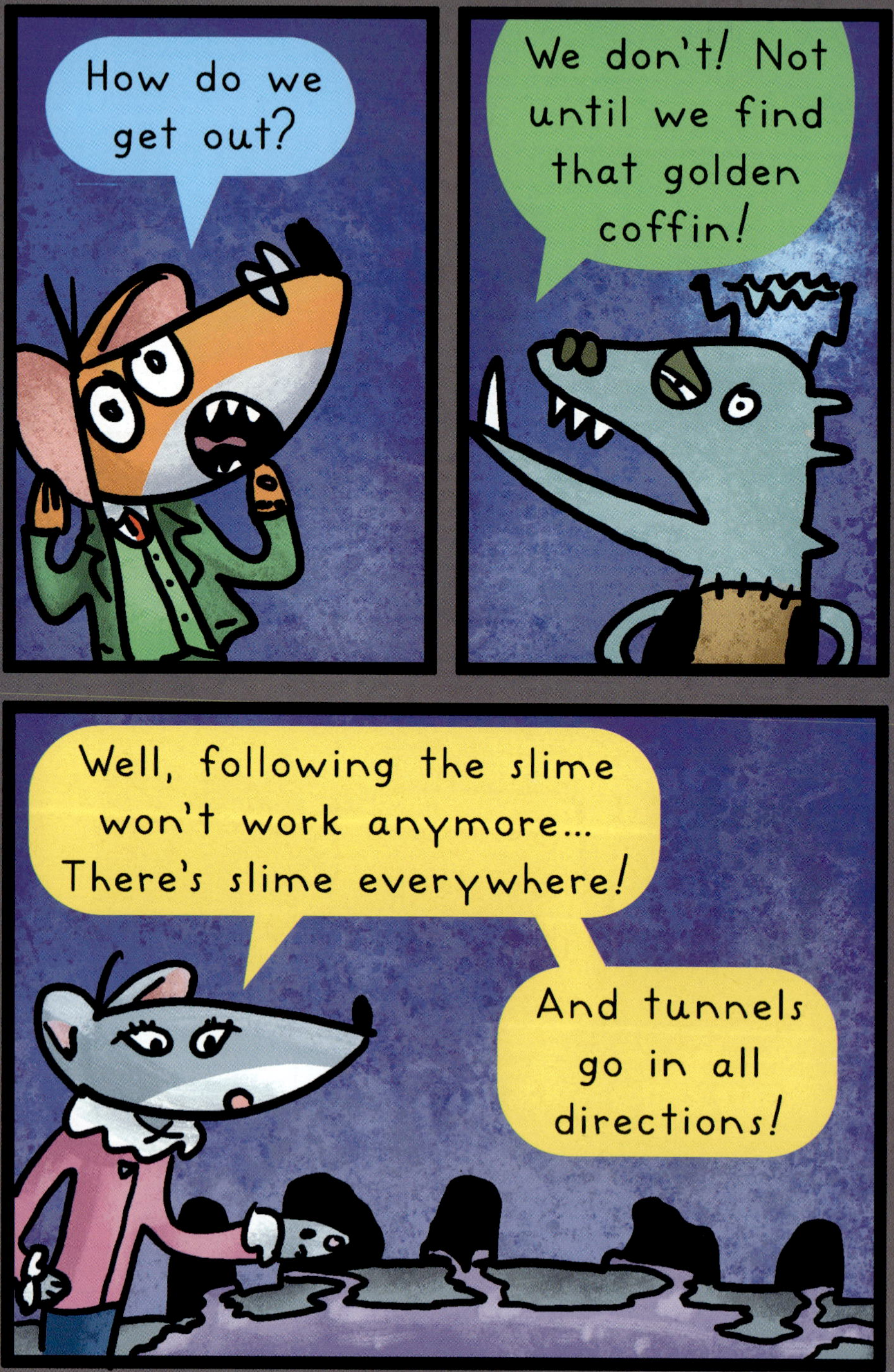

Well, following the slime won't work anymore... There's slime everywhere!

And tunnels go in all directions!

We'll have to split up...
I'll go with you, Creepella!
Aw, you're all so sweet, but I think I'll go with Geronimo... 
Grumble!
Why me?

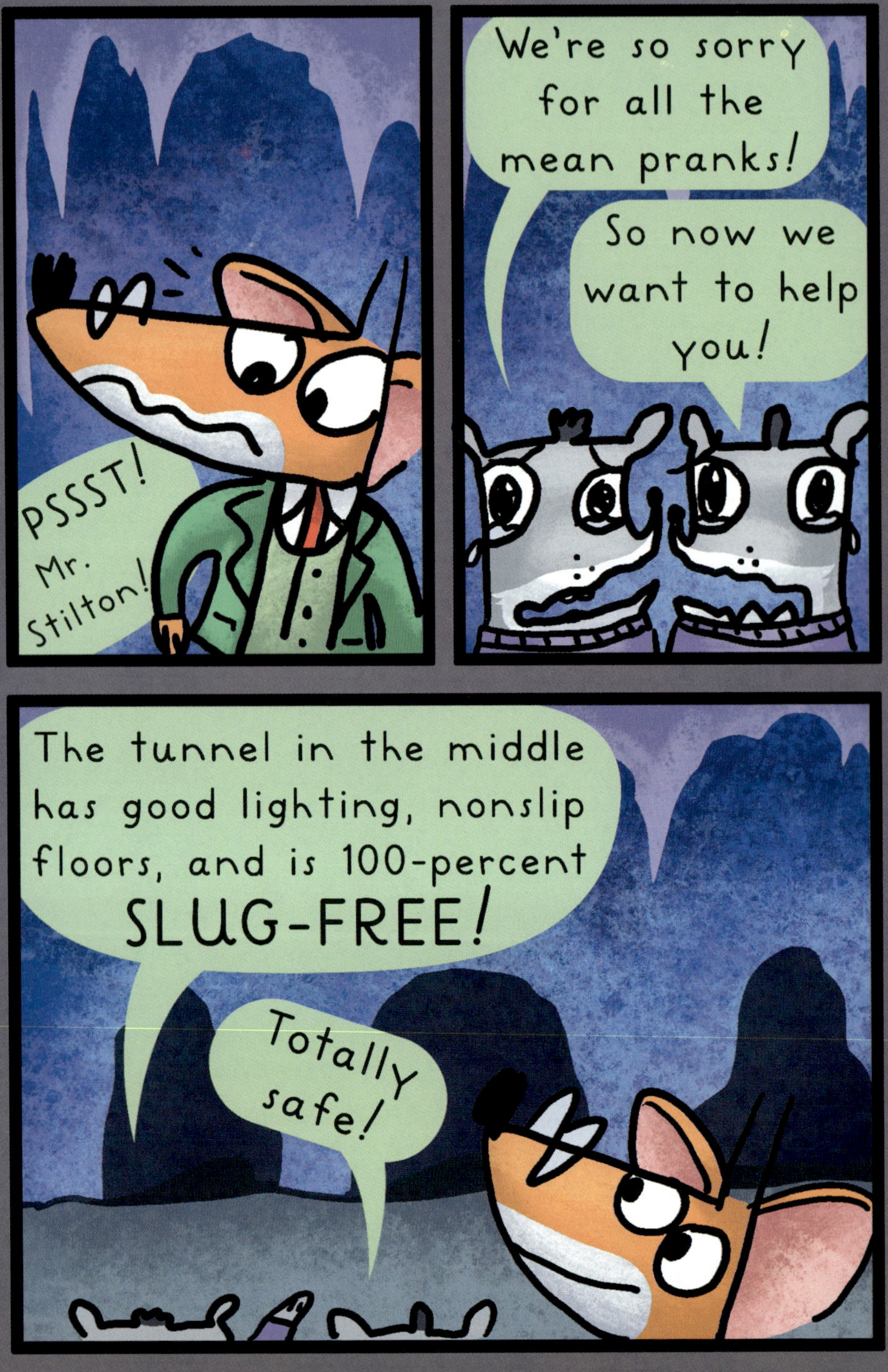

The tunnel in the middle has good lighting, nonslip floors, and is 100-percent SLUG-FREE!

Totally safe!

Thanks, boys! I knew you couldn't be all bad!

Oh, Creepella, let's try this one!

Nice work, Snip.
Couldn't have done it without you, Snap!

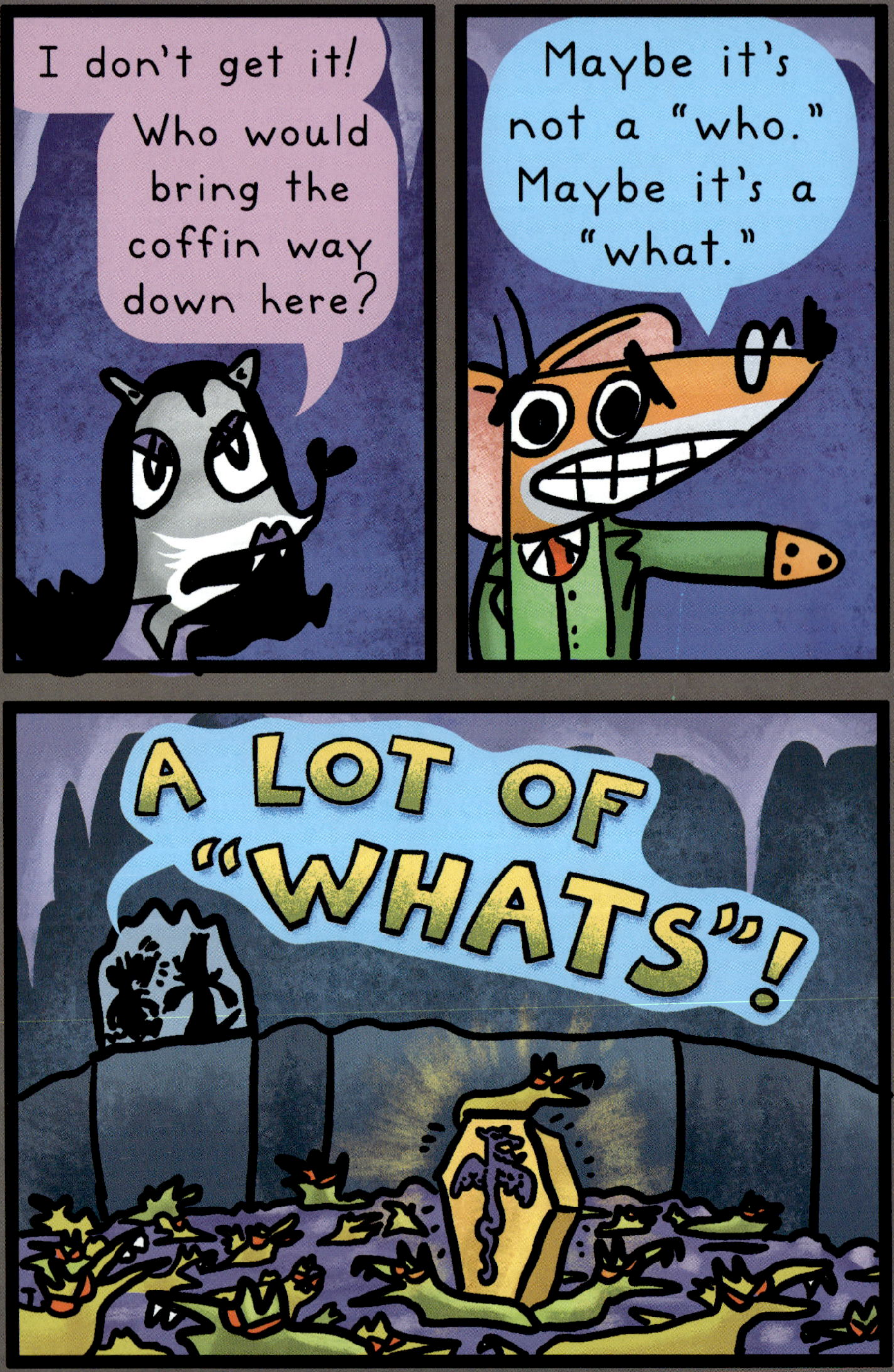

A LOT OF "WHATS"!

I was scared! I was terrified! I was ready to get my TAIL out of there! I took a step back...

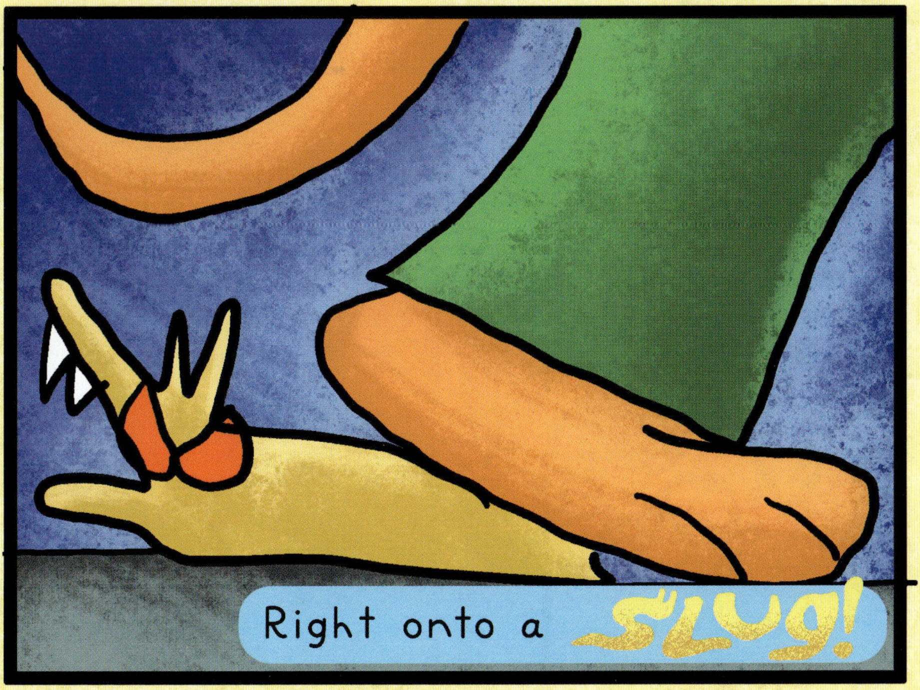

Right onto a SLUG!

Whooooops!
SQUISH!

Oof!
BONK

OH NO!
TOTTER

AAAAAAAAAH!

Oh, Gerrykins! You're so brave to rush into the slug pit to save the coffin!

Remember... they're harmless!

(Until midnight.)

And then...

...from far, far above...

...through a mile of stone...

...from the castle...

...through the caves...

...came the sound I feared most...

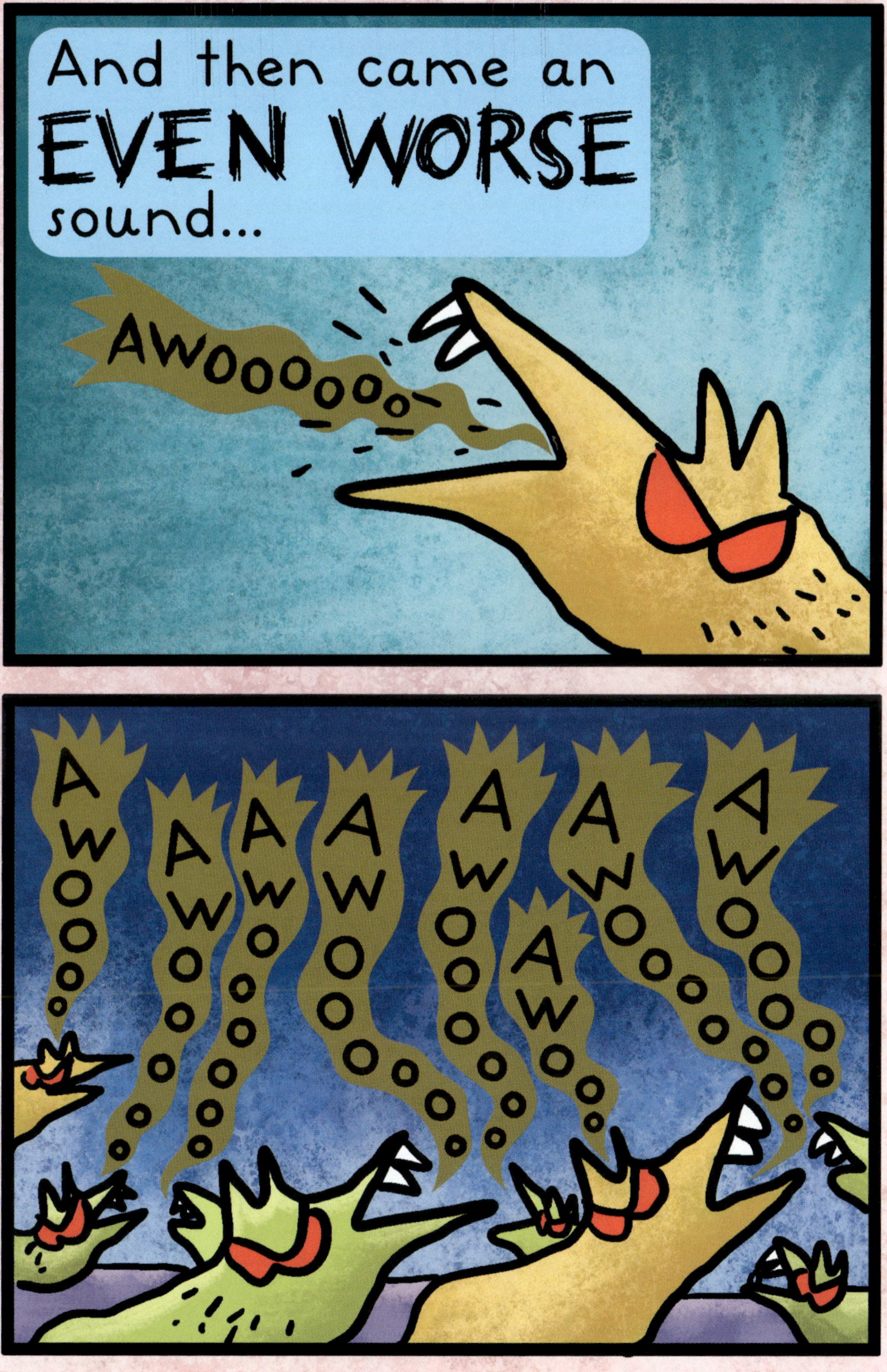

And then came an **EVEN WORSE** sound...

AWOOOOOOO

The slugs began climbing on one another...

...melting into one another...

becoming...

CHAPTER TWENTY-EIGHT

WHAT A DISGUSTING mouse!

Instead of five thousand slugs, I was now facing one slug that was five thousand times bigger!

I tried to climb out of the pit...

Darling... take my hand!

But it was too steep and slimy!

Just when I had given up hope...
there was a voice in the darkness.

It was Trap! And... Bob? Somehow they had found another entrance to the pit! But to me, it was an **EXIT!**

...scooping up the coffin...

...making a MIGHTY LEAP for the exit!

It was almost as good a jump as Perry Miscus could do!!!

ALMOST!

YELP!

The wereslug had me in its slimy claws!

HOLEY HEADCHEESE!*

*Headcheese is not a kind of cheese. It's actually something almost as gross as this wereslug!!!

I had slime for dinner.

Now slime is having me for dinner!

Suddenly, it stopped and SNIFFED...

Instantly, it turned back into five thousand small slugs... who all slithered away, gagging...

NASTY!
YUK!
Dude, what was that stink?
Glak!
Groan!
Luckily, I have a cold.
P.U.!
Blech!
I almost BARFED!
Grody to the max!
What a disgusting mouse!
Gagorama!

H'yuk! H'yuk!

Gee, Cuz, you must smell slightly worse than normal!

It's not me!!!!!! I think it's something in my pocket!

I pulled out... Thea's uneaten mystery giblet!

Could it really smell that bad?
SNIFF

Yes.

CLONK

CHAPTER TWENTY-NINE

SO SORRY, GERRYKINS!

I was having a beautiful dream!
My novel was a bestseller!
The title was...

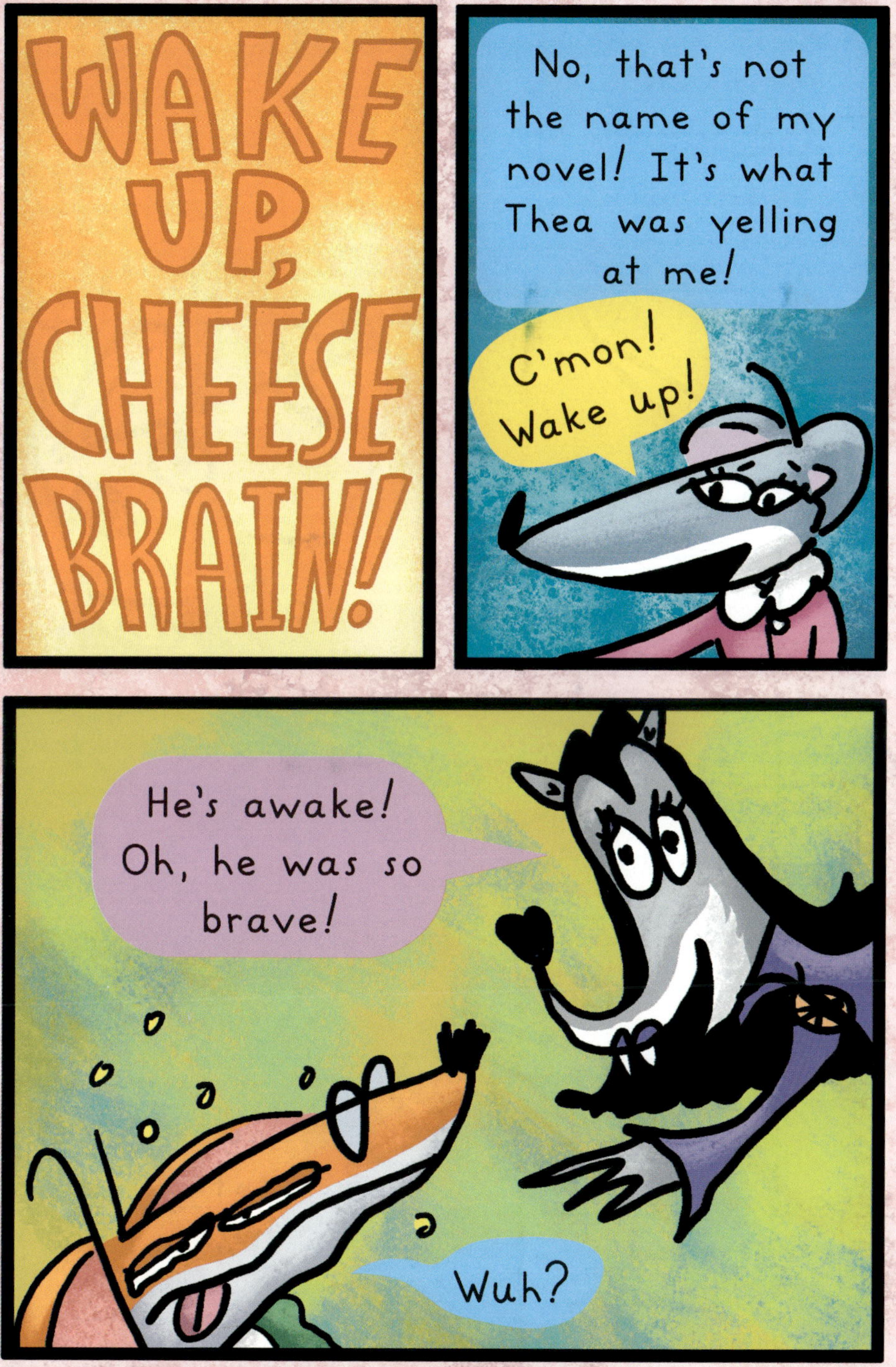

He's awake! Oh, he was so brave!

Wuh?

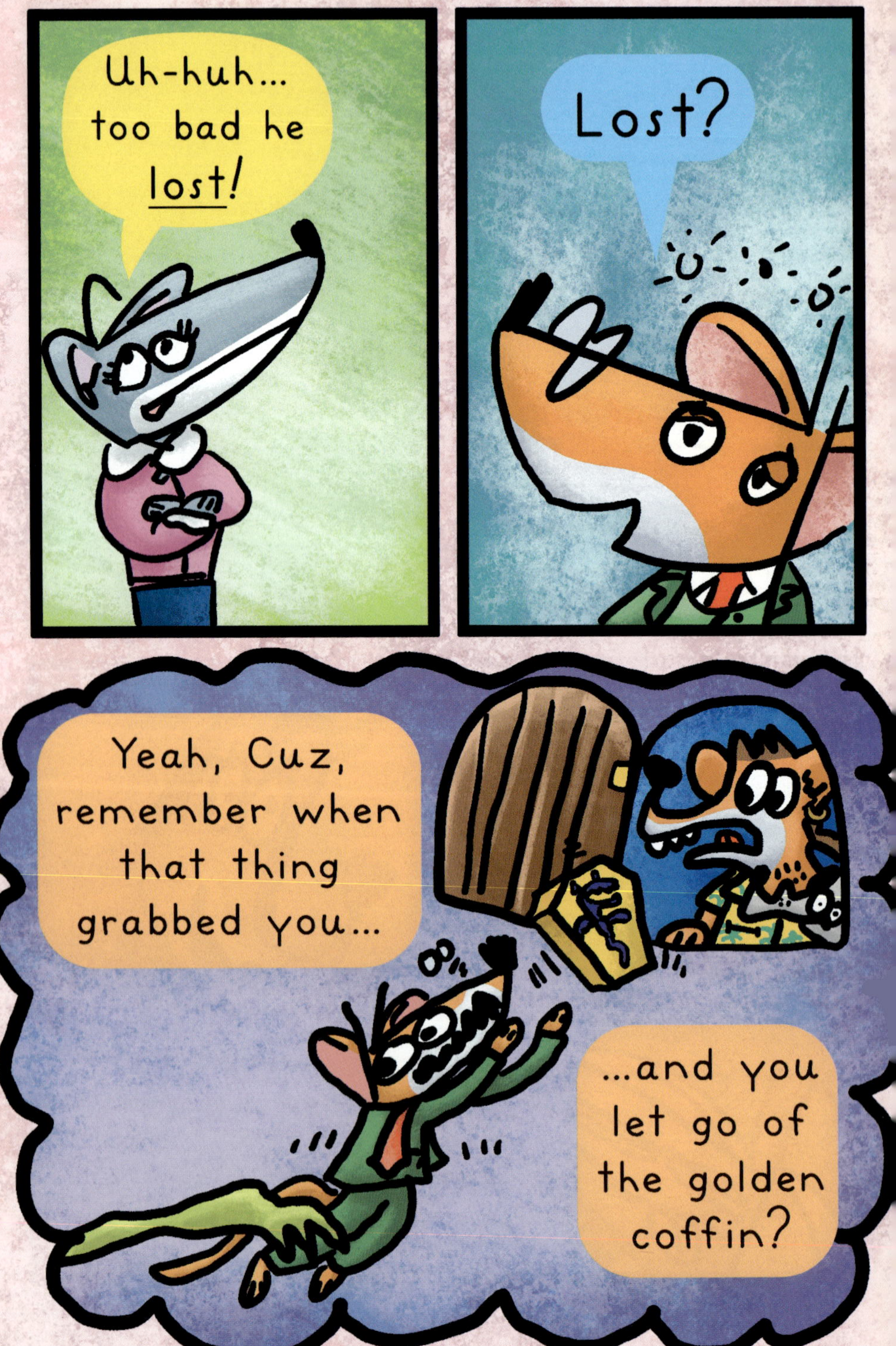

Yeah, Cuz, remember when that thing grabbed you...

...and you let go of the golden coffin?

Well, Bob here caught it!

I'm surprisingly nimble.

So sorry, Gerrykins! But Bob gets to go on the Transratania adventure with me...

I'm so happy!

Uh... for Bob, I mean... since he loves... uh... danger and adventure... and uh...

Can I go home now?

Don't be silly, Gerrykins. Not until we have DESSERT!

THE END

EPILOGUE

One day, my assistant, Pinky Pick, came running into my office waving her phone.

Oh,
FABULOUS FETA!
My new book is a bestseller!
SLIME'S RHYMES!
Is it... number one?
Uh... not exactly.

Number two?
Not quite...

Top ten?
...er...

Top twenty?
Uh-uh.

Top 100??
SOB
Well, what is it?

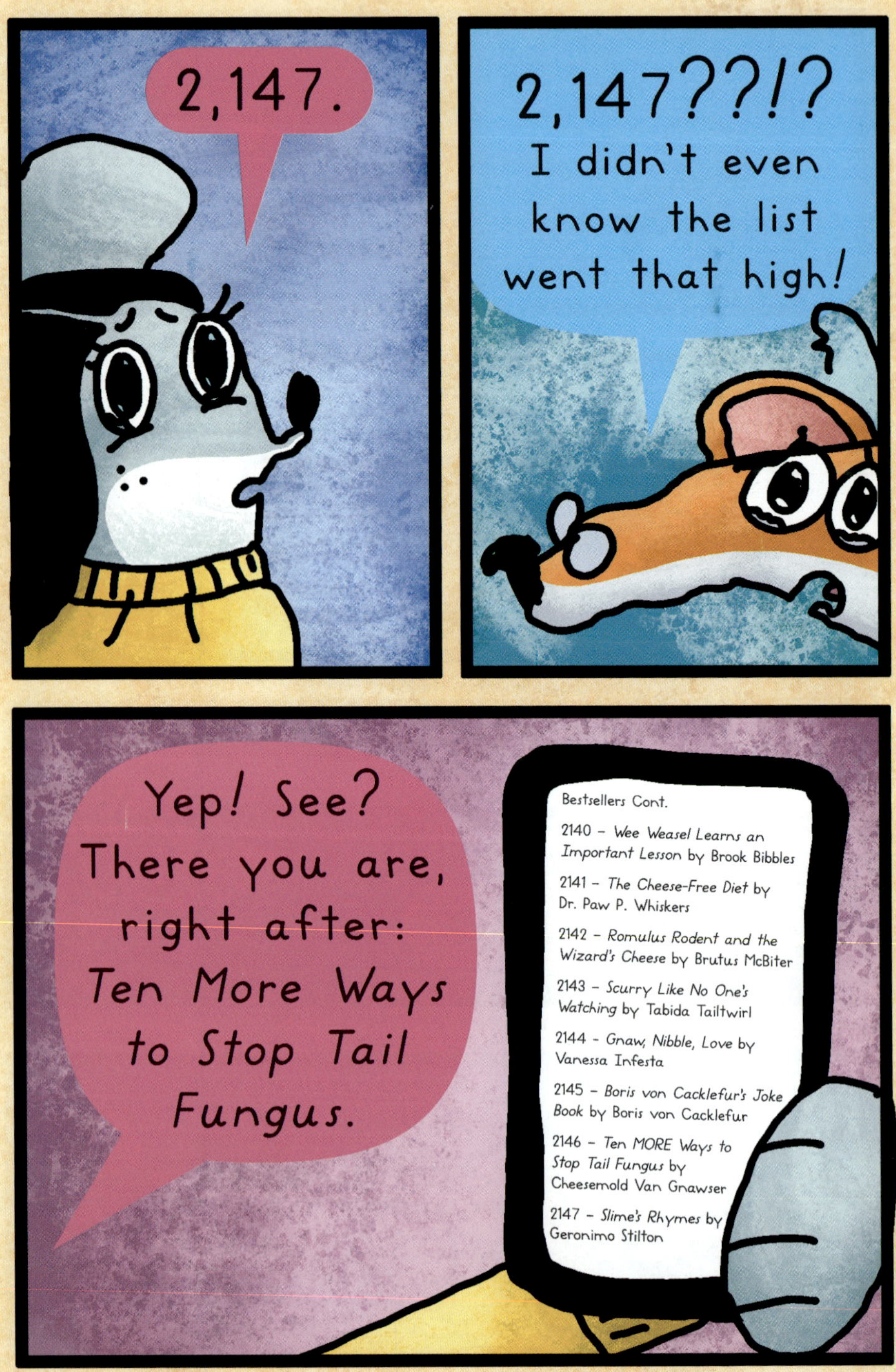

Yep! See? There you are, right after: Ten More Ways to Stop Tail Fungus.

Bestsellers Cont.

2140 – *Wee Weasel Learns an Important Lesson* by Brook Bibbles

2141 – *The Cheese-Free Diet* by Dr. Paw P. Whiskers

2142 – *Romulus Rodent and the Wizard's Cheese* by Brutus McBiter

2143 – *Scurry Like No One's Watching* by Tabida Tailtwirl

2144 – *Gnaw, Nibble, Love* by Vanessa Infesta

2145 – *Boris von Cacklefur's Joke Book* by Boris von Cacklefur

2146 – *Ten MORE Ways to Stop Tail Fungus* by Cheesemold Van Gnawser

2147 – *Slime's Rhymes* by Geronimo Stilton

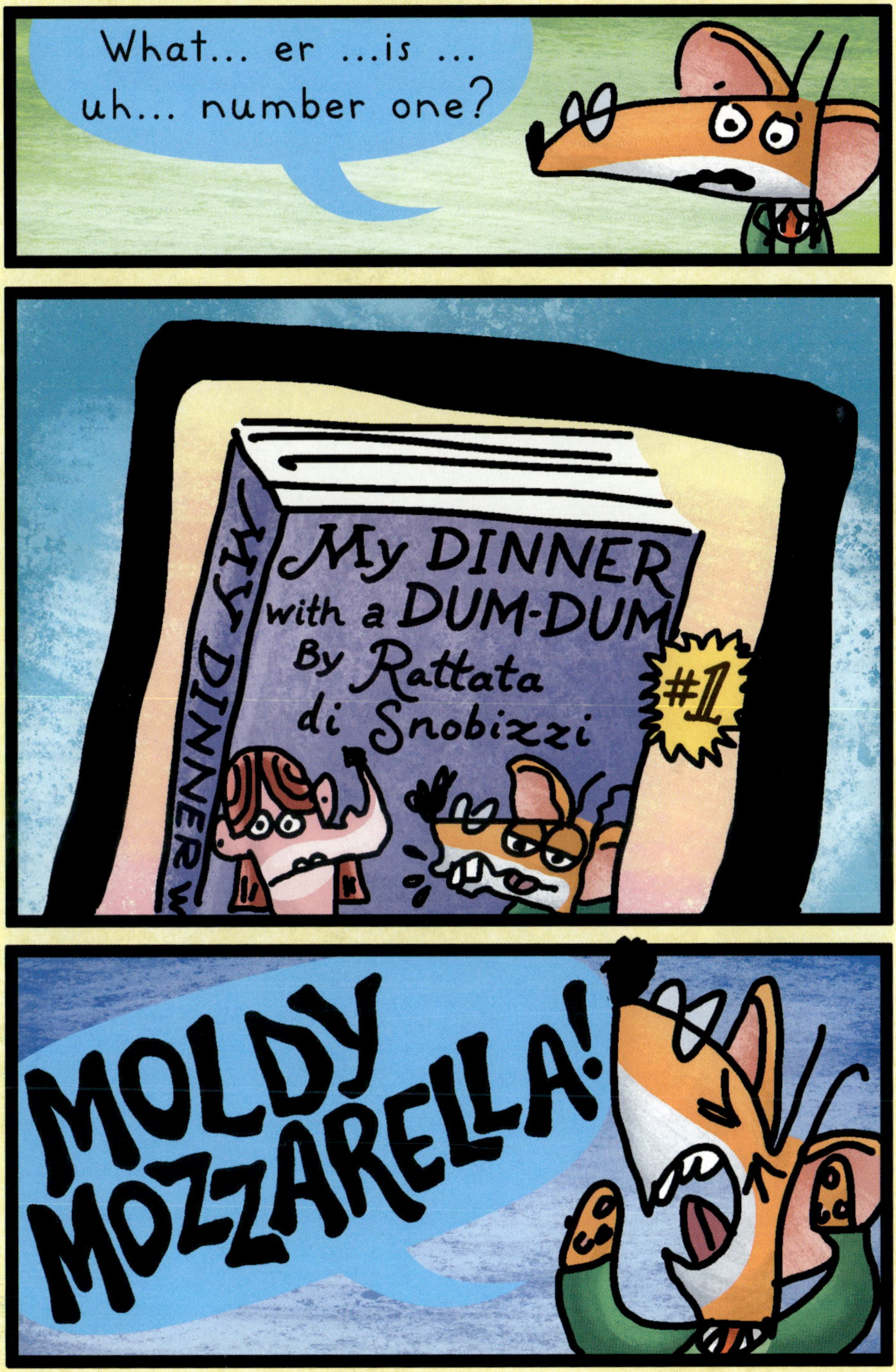

My DINNER with a DUM-DUM
By Rattata di Snobizzi
#1
MY DINNER W

GREETINGS FROM TRANSRATANIA!

Dearest Gerry,

So sorry you're missing out! The tombs are lovely this time of year! And lucky Bob has already seen three vampires and a ghoul! Best of all, the Swamp Bat Festival begins next week!

xoxo,
CREEPELLA

Geronimo
Stilton
RODENT'S GAZETTE
NEW MOUSE CITY
MOUSE ISLAND

DON'T MISS ANY ORIGINAL

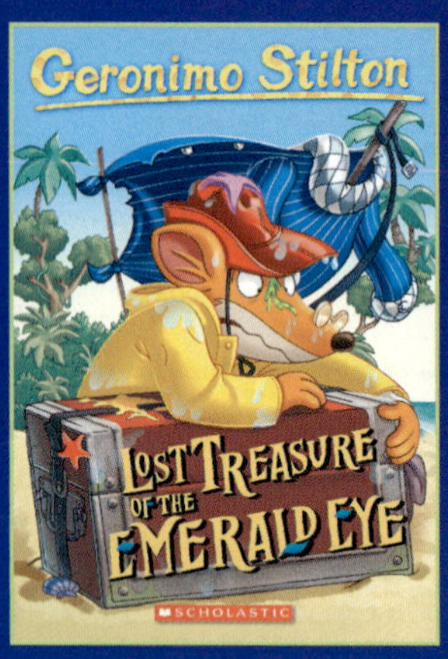

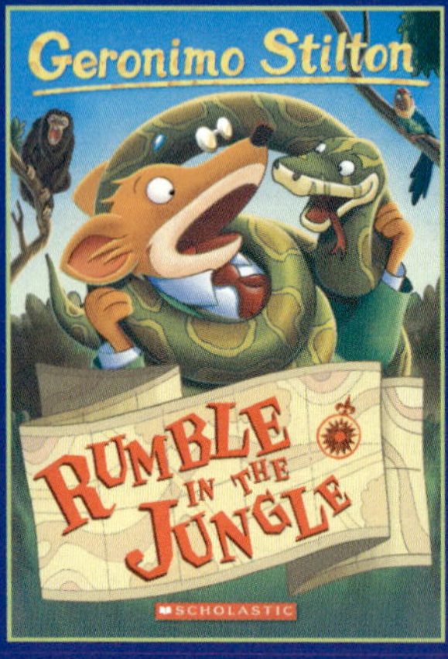

OF GERONIMO'S ADVENTURES!

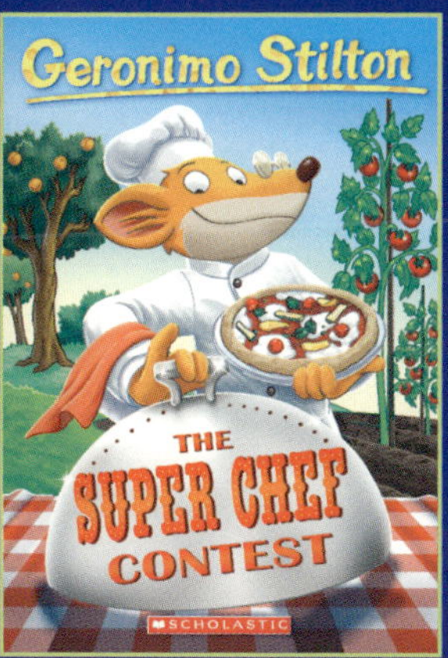

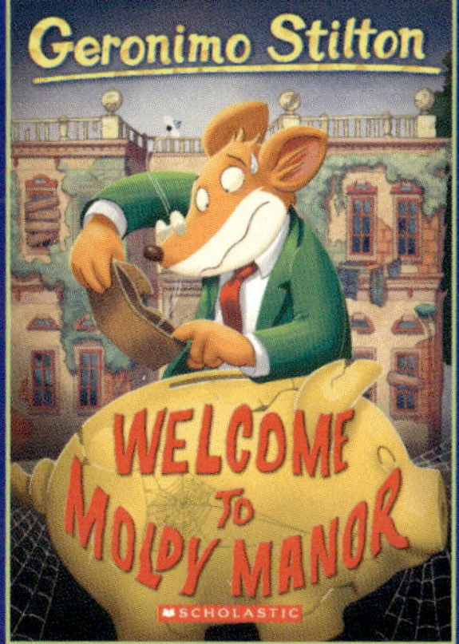

Geronimo Stilton

is an author and the editor-in-chief of *The Rodent's Gazette*, New Mouse City's most popular newspaper. He was awarded the Ratitzer Prize for his investigative journalism and the Anderson 2000 Prize for Personality of the Year. His books have been published all over the world. He loves to spend all his spare time with his family and friends.

Elisabetta Dami was born in Milan, Italy, and is the daughter of a book publisher. She loves adventures of all kinds, all over the world: She has piloted small planes and parachuted, climbed Mount Kilimanjaro, trekked in Nepal, run the New York City Marathon three times, and visited wildlife reservations in Africa where she had close encounters with elephants and gorillas . . . But she believes books are the greatest adventure, and this is why she created Geronimo Stilton!

Tom Angleberger is the author of lots of books about talking animals, talking plants, and even a piece of talking paper, namely Origami Yoda. Since middle school, he has drawn countless comics and cartoons but this is the first time he has drawn a whole graphic novel. He lives in the mountains of Virginia with his wife, Cece Bell, who has also drawn a graphic novel, *El Deafo*.

Corey Barba is a Los Angeles–based cartoonist, writer, and musician. As a kid, he loved monsters, cartoons, puppets, and mad scientists. As an adult, he combines all those things in his work every day. In addition to coloring books for Scholastic, he has worked for DreamWorks Animation, SpongeBob Comics, *MAD* magazine, and lots of other fun stuff!

Don't miss the next graphic novel by me, **Geronimo Stilton**

Feta* not miss it!

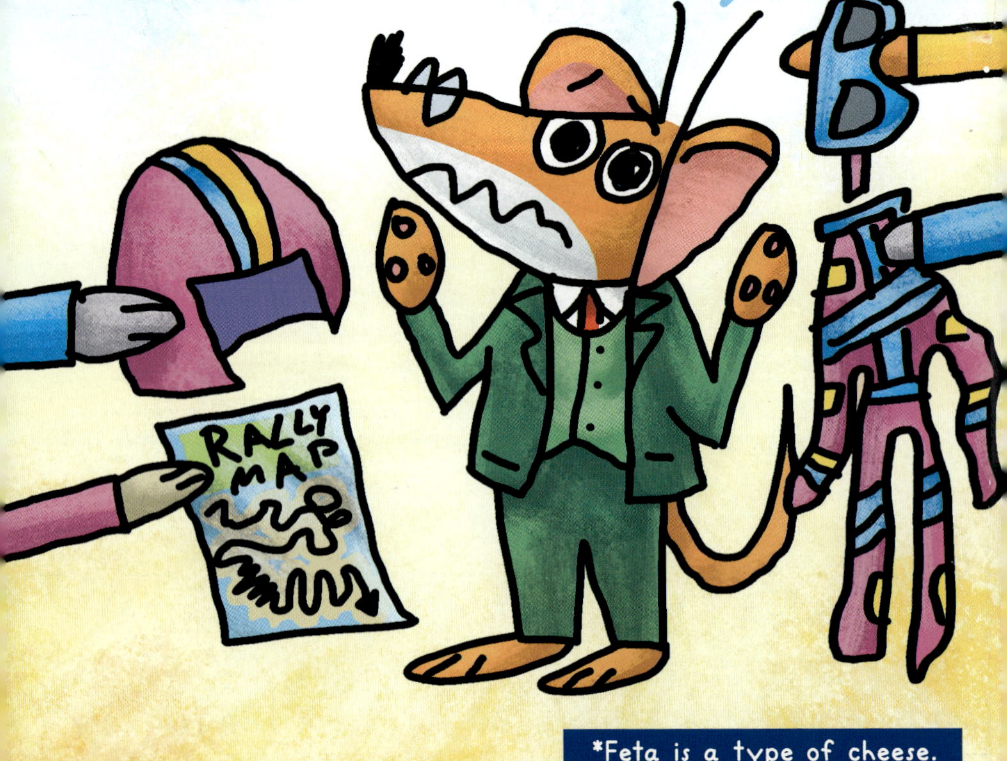

*Feta is a type of cheese.